The Preservation of the Agile Heart

Agile Heart

From Mindset to Consciousness

Jean Richardson

The Preservation of the Agile Heart: From Mindset to
Consciousness
by Jean Richardson

Azure Gate Press

First Edition 2018

First E-book 2017

Published in the United States by Azure Gate Press, 3857 SE
41st Ave., Portland, Oregon 97202

Cover designed by: Meghan Lewis | melewdesign.com

e-book ISBN: 978-1-61083-005-8 Library of Congress
Cataloging-in-Publication Data

Richardson, Jean 1962 -

The Preservation of the Agile Heart: From Mindset to
Consciousness by Jean Richardson. -- 1st ed.

Includes bibliographical references.

Summary: "Agile transformations in organizations and teams
are explored as a personal process that are best led by agilists
who are on the transformational path toward agile consciousness
themselves."

Contents

Dedication

To my friend, Phyllis Thompson, without whose quiet support during the drafting of this book I may not have gone on.

And, for my dog Frankie, who probably thinks I've changed his name to "Writing! Go lie down."

Acknowledgements

Authors always thank so many people. There is a reason for that. They learn in the process of writing a book how much help they need, moral and material, in order to bring even a small book to print.

The following individuals read early versions of this book and gave me much needed feedback which provided long nights of hard thought and made this a better book: Phyllis Thompson, Valerie D'Sa-Mayer, Allan Combs, Aaron Vannatter, Jerry Weinberg, Karl Wiegers, Daniel Ackermann, Matt Horvat, Dave Gipp, April Mills, Rony Lerner, Pat Reed, Jackie Barretta, Shane Hastie, Ashish Vaidya, and Kymm Nelsen.

And, to Mark Klein: Thanks for meeting for coffee. I hope this answers the question.

Writing is lonely work, which is why I have such a love/hate relationship with it. I remember hearing another writer say in an interview some years ago that writers are boring people. Basically, they're good at staying indoors. Thanks to everyone who helped me stay indoors long enough to write this book, particularly Valerie.

Introduction

This book is about the problem of agile transformations in organizations and teams. This book is for those people who desire and advocate for those transformations. They are agile coaches, agile consultants, agile advocates, agile champions, and are sometimes also called Scrum Masters. This book is for the experienced agilist, not the beginner. And, I shall say more about that later.

I decided years ago that if I ever wrote a book, I would not want to write a big, fat tome, or "bible." The bookstores are full of books that claim to be complete and authoritative. Many of them are certainly *thick*. This makes them forbidding for many readers. I wanted to write a book you could fit in your pocket to read on the train. At the very least, something short enough that you could read it over the weekend. I wrote this book with that goal in mind, among others.

The Challenge: Develop Yourself

There are a number of concepts, ideas, and sources I employ here that I do not go into in great depth. The early reviewers of this book all noted the advanced nature of the text. That is intentional: This is not a book for people who are new to the agile movement. It is for agile coaches and advocates who have seen failed and flagging adoptions and are wondering what to do about it. I make the case that the focus needs to be back on ourselves, on self-transformation before organizational transformation. This is best done in the shelter of each other as it is difficult work. At some point, though, this is deeply personal work, like birthing and dying. Though others may be present, this is something that we must be personally and fundamentally engaged in.

The Challenge: Develop Yourself

In the pursuit of brevity, I have chosen to sacrifice the lengthy discussions required to fully describe the depth I am only describing superficially. However, I have done my best to provide footnotes, endnotes, and a bibliography that will assist you in educating yourself more thoroughly on whatever particularly intrigues you enough to "go look it up" as my mother used to say to me when, as a child, I would ask her what a word or concept meant. That was why we had a multi-volume dictionary and three sets of encyclopedias—so we could "go look it up" and educate ourselves.

I do not tend to write about things about which one can be authoritative. That is, perhaps, part of their charm for me. This book is not authoritative and doesn't claim to be. But, hopefully, it will engage you enough that you will want to read it on the train and complete the reading of it in a single weekend, or maybe even overnight. If so, I will be glad. Here's hoping!

Ultimately, this book is an invitation to a conversation. One thing that kept me from writing a book for years is that books tend to become "set in stone," even though we may provide future editions or updates. A person reads a book and walks away with those ideas, at that moment in time, within them. They don't tend to check back to see how the author's learning is progressing. I've published many conference papers, articles, and blog posts over the last 30 years. I strive to keep learning and developing my thinking and practice. My understanding and practice change. There is more to come.

You will see me use the term "agilist" throughout this book. I use this term to describe anyone using any agile methods, aspiring to agility in their lives or work, or appreciating and attempting to implement the Agile Manifesto and Principles. I use the term generously, and that is my intention.

Introduction

Several months ago, a colleague used the term "radical inclusivity" in a conversation we were having about diversity, and I was interested enough in the term to do some digging.* In my exploration I came across a tremendously valuable little book, *Radical Inclusivity: Expanding Our Minds Beyond Dualistic Thinking* by Jeff Carreira. Jeff's book in no small way motivated me to write this book. I had been thinking about these ideas for years, and they have been coming to a head for me in the last year or so. Not only does Carreira provide the best discussion I've seen of dualistic versus non-dualistic consciousness and the difficulty of moving between them, but just as Jean Gebser, through his life's work as a poet and consciousness researcher, and Alan Combs, professor and author of *Consciousness Explained Better*, have done, he points to the value of poetry in tipping us over the edge from our current consciousness to the next level. "Poetry allows for enough ambiguity of meaning to allow it to become a launch pad beyond the consciousness inherent in the language being used."[1]

As a poet, I have a deep-seated sense of, and commitment to, the social and evolutionary value of poetry. As a software development professional, I have been present for countless poetic moments in organizations, moments which we often overlook because the lookers have no notion of what they are seeing or its value. There is always a poetic aspect to human endeavor, and agile is about human endeavor. You will see me use poetry throughout this book to help you move to understandings that could take many pages to convey otherwise or to deeply seat a concept I'm asking you to consider.

While agile thinking and the frameworks and practices that agilists use have evolved quite a bit in the last seventeen years, the Agile Manifesto and Principles have not. Some people object to

---

* For a discussion of this, see my blog post at http://azuregate.net/2017/02/26/ consciousness-as-a-continuity-radical-inclusivity-and-the-art-of-staying-on-the-inside/

The Challenge: Develop Yourself

this. The Modern Agile[2] folks are making a strong case that a new manifesto is required. During a conversation last summer at one of the local agile community discussion groups I facilitate, fifty or so of us sat down over lunch and talked about the wisdom of having a new manifesto—or not. We decided that the Agile Manifesto and the Modern Agile Manifesto could coexist just fine, the first for software related activities and products, the second for "the business side," which can be a catch-all for "everyone who is not us."

I would not want to see the Agile Manifesto and Principles go away any time soon. I am interested to see a new manifesto, propounded in 2014, by the Responsive Organization movement (see Appendix B for a discussion of that manifesto). It looks a lot like the Agile Manifesto. It deserves airtime, as well.

But, for this book, I'd like to recapitulate the Agile Manifesto and Principles here in full. I'm often surprised how many agilists have never read the Agile Manifesto and Principles. As you continue reading, you may have cause to consider what I'm claiming here in the context of the specific wording of those documents. You could go look them up at www.agilemanifesto. org. But, just in case that's not sufficiently easy to do, you have them here and can just flip back, read them and cogitate on them a bit.

Manifesto for Agile Software Development[†]

We are uncovering better ways of developing
software by doing it and helping others do it.
Through this work we have come to value:

Individuals and interactions over processes and tools
Working software over comprehensive documentation
Customer collaboration over contract negotiation
Responding to change over following a plan

That is, while there is value in the items on
the right, we value the items on the left more.

Kent Beck	James Grenning	Robert C. Martin
Mike Beedle	Jim Highsmith	Steve Mellor
Arie van Bennekum	Andrew Hunt	Ken Schwaber
Alistair Cockburn	Ron Jeffries	Jeff Sutherland
Ward Cunningham	Jon Kern	Dave Thomas
Martin Fowler	Brian Marick	

Principles behind the Agile Manifesto

We follow these principles:
Our highest priority is to satisfy the customer through early and
continuous delivery of valuable software.

Welcome changing requirements, even late in development.
Agile processes harness change for the customer's competitive
advantage.

Deliver working software frequently, from a couple of weeks to a
couple of months, with a preference to the shorter timescale.

[†] © 2001, the above authors this declaration may be freely copied in any form,
but only in its entirety through this notice.

Principles behind the Agile Manifesto

Business people and developers must work together daily throughout the project.

Build projects around motivated individuals. Give them the environment and support they need, and trust them to get the job done.

The most efficient and effective method of conveying information to and within a development team is face-to-face conversation.

Working software is the primary measure of progress.

Agile processes promote sustainable development. The sponsors, developers, and users should be able to maintain a constant pace indefinitely.

Continuous attention to technical excellence and good design enhances agility.

Simplicity—the art of maximizing the amount of work not done— is essential.

The best architectures, requirements, and designs emerge from self-organizing teams.

At regular intervals, the team reflects on how to become more effective, then tunes and adjusts its behavior accordingly.

What is Agile?

Even experienced agilists can differ on this question. So, know that, for the purposes of this book, "agile" is any way of organizing work or orienting toward people that fits into the context of the manifesto and principles above. Yes, it's a broad territory and goes beyond Scrum, Kanban, and Extreme Programming.

Chapter 1: Why This? Why Now?

For the last few years, I have become increasingly concerned about the state of the agile movement. It was clear to me that we have become quite good at discussing very basic topics and inquiring into nits. We are masterly at explaining away our failures and saying, essentially, "look over there not over here" and that things were harder than we expected them to be. Simultaneously, we are too often quite unkind to each other when one of us experiences failure or even a misstep in behavior, which makes us less likely to reach out to each other for support in our development. Perfection is not an attractive teacher for the broken. Ritual brokenness is not an attractive teacher for the thinking person. I began to wonder whether the agile movement could be transformed or if it would simply have to die away, as so many other movements have.

How I Heard About the Agile Movement

The genesis of this small book, or monograph, as Sherlock Holmes would have called it, was an email or a phone call I received over 15 years ago after making a presentation summarizing my class on Collaboration for Cross-Functional Teams to the Rose City Software Process Improvement Network (SPIN) at Oregon Graduate Institute in Hillsboro, Oregon. I no longer remember whether I received a phone call or an email, but I do remember the caller‡ said, "we think you're one of us." Then the caller asked me if I'd like to come to dinner at his house to meet Norm Kerth. Not knowing who Norm was but being very eager to find out who thought I was one of them, since affinity groups are precious, I made my way out to the suburbs of Portland, Oregon, where I live, to meet Norm and his host.

To this day, there are only two people who inspire something akin to hero worship in me: Nikki Giovanni, a feisty African

---

‡ The caller is intentionally not identified in this text, as is his preference.

How I Heard About the Agile Movement

American poet, and Norm Kerth, author of the first comprehensive book on software project retrospectives. The "we" that someone thought I was a part of was the agile community, a small group, at that time, marching staunchly under the flag of the Agile Manifesto and Principles Behind the Agile Manifesto.

Slowly, I realized that another presentation I had heard a few years before by Ward Cunningham on an approach to software development called Extreme Programming, was also about agile. It may have been at that moment that I was hooked because the team I was working with then was one of the happiest and most productive teams I'd ever worked on. We attended the presentation together and realized that much of what he was talking about in terms of team dynamics, we were already doing.

Our Consciousness is at Issue

As I sit here at my desk this evening in June of 2017, I look back on many years of practice, the hopes many of us had for the agile movement, and many learnings along the way.

I first outlined this book in the months following the publication of an article I co-authored on consciousness hacking[3] through the use of certain technical practices. That article was published September 1, 2016. During its development and the months of reflection since, I learned much about the nature of my own thinking and realized the degree to which it diverged from that which has become the mainstream among agilists. The more I struggled to make my thinking clear, the more I came to understand how aligned it is with that of other people. They often are familiar with both adaptive and predictive ways of organizing work as well as power-sharing and authoritarian ways of relating to people who are trying to get things done.

Many of these people see that the reach of the agile movement has exceeded its grasp. But the reason it has, I believe, has little

Chapter 1: Why This? Why Now?

to do with how we organize work. It has far more to do with how we have agreed to approach agility when we—and here I mean the agile advocates, champions, and agile coaches—contract with clients and introduce agile methods and thinking in organizations. I have come to see the dominant paradigm among mainstream agilists as more mechanistic than is good for us and more mechanistic than we acknowledge.

Over the last few years I began to realize that the agile community had come to resemble the traditional business community in a remarkable number of ways. Three frameworks discussed and applied most often, Scrum, XP, and Kanban, appear to be constraining our understanding of agility. However, we really don't have a good way of engaging in necessary conversations without using the usual language: Product Owner, Product Manager, product ownership, team, Scrum Master, manager, Project Manager.

Some agilists focused only at the team system level while others preferred to focus at the enterprise level. However, both were apparently looking at laying a framework down to change minds by changing the structure of the system. Though, some agile coaches and consultants appreciate and advocate for practice and pattern-based approaches rather than out-of-the-box frameworks.

I am always cautious about whole systems transformations led by essentially external actors. A decade and a half ago, someone close to me was caught in an organizational redesign process in preparation for a corporate sale that coincided with a number of voluntary terminations, one suicide, and my friend's nervous breakdown. I had been approached to be part of that organizational redesign team, and I was very glad I had not moved forward with that opportunity. Ever since, I have had a certain sensitivity to redesigning organizations and reshuffling teams and

Our Consciousness is at Issue

the possible outcomes of such changes. Change that comes from outside and is imposed on others, especially the kind of large-scale organizational change we've seen so much of in the last few decades, can have cascading effects that the change agents rarely consider and even more rarely can predict.

We are at a time when our social and organizing competencies are outmatched by the challenges before us. We want more individual freedom, and we are frightened by what personal accountability can mean as our social systems are currently organized. All of us, at least most days, want to survive. And if we are to survive, we need to find new and more effective ways of organizing work and orienting toward people. Fifteen years ago, agile held great promise, to me as it did to so many others. Since then, I have witnessed and been part of a range of efforts that, to my knowledge, while they did not result in suicides or nervous breakdowns, they did, for a range of reasons, result in pain for the reorganized souls.

In any change effort, there are those who see, or believe they see, the way ahead, and there will be those who don't see things the same way at all. Within the duration of the life of the Agile Manifesto, we have seen a range of things occur: Two major recessions, one based on over-valued tech stocks and one based on over-valued real estate; the grounding of all commercial air traffic in the US after an attack on New York City; several globally publicized genocides; the rise of climate change; the emergence of global pandemics which require constant vigilance; escalating complexity in software systems; the emergence of software as a key driving force behind government and almost all enterprises; the actuality of cyberwarfare; and the intercontinental grasp of globalization—to name just a few recent historical incidents. All of us are now dealing with the kind of complexity that software teams were dealing with at the founding of the agile movement. Many of us see the pursuit of agility as the means to living

Chapter 1: Why This? Why Now?

successfully now. As first coined by the military[4] , we live in a volatile, uncertain, complex, and ambiguous VUCA world. And, in this VUCA world, some of us reach out with hope and lusting curiosities for ways of coping and engaging in the world to preserve the human experience while retaining and extending prosperity. This is not easy.

While many of us once turned to agile as a context setting frame for a better experience in the world of work, now many of the original developers and signers of the manifesto have moved on in dismay. Increasingly, individual practitioners and manifesto signers cry out against the increased mechanistic feel of the agile movement. Agile, as a movement, seems to have stopped learning, in a manner of speaking. Some would ascribe this to the emergence of large consultancies, productized practices, licensing of new approaches, and multi-million-dollar consulting careers.

Whatever the cause, much that inspires seems to be beyond the bounds of common agile practice these days. And so, many of us are noticing the boundaries around the community and the cultural precepts that preserve those boundaries. We find we have been all too willing to adulate heroes who play their air guitars to distract us from our own personal lack of transformation.

And personal transformation, many of us have come to realize, is what agile transformation is all about. The scope of the needed transformation is as great as that described by Combs in *Consciousness Explained Better*:

> *A mental perspectival understanding of the snow would specify when it fell according to clock time. "It snowed between three and five o'clock this morning." But an integral experience of the snow might emphasize that it is, "The night's snow; the gift of the night," or some other poetic representation*

Our Consciousness is at Issue

emphasizing the quality of the experience of the night and the snow, rather than abstracting an event outside of experience that presumably occurred during a particular episode of clock time. (Combs, pg. 75)

The practice of Agile may, and hopefully will, change, but the essence of it is unlikely to die or go away. However, next level or new consciousness level, new ways of orienting to people and work, such as agile, succeed only if we ourselves transform. Only personal transformation results in true organizational transformation. This may be what was underlying the romantic nature of the agile movement all along. We the people, who spend so much of our lives at work, and we in knowledge work in particular, seek a freedom of spirit we don't know. But we believe our work can get us there, can help transform us or actualize us. For us, the work is personal, and so, I will argue throughout this book, the transformation must be, as well.

The poet Mary Oliver asks us a resounding question:

Tell me, what is it you plan to do
with your one wild and precious life?[5]

For agile coaches, champions, and advocates, there is a why inside that question, and after the "why" a certain kind of "how."

But what drew us to agile in the first place? And, how do we pursue and preserve what brought at least some of us here? That is what this book explores. Come along!

Chapter 2: The Agile Journey Is Personal

In April of 2017 I published a LinkedIn article[6] as a way of thinking about the ineffable in agile and getting a broader view. I asked the readers what they thought people were advocating for when they advocate for Agile—specific business and technical practices notwithstanding. The article received hundreds of views and a number of comments. Two, in particular, were interesting. One person said,

From what I can gather from the article and in your subsequent reply to what exactly you are looking for as response to the question is, why do some sing praises of Agile as if singing "Hare Rama Hare Krishna".

This response charmed me because it captured the flavor of some conversations I've witnessed or been a party to quite perfectly. Another thoughtful reader said,

When I teach or coach Agile I always refer to my "passion" about the subject, and maybe that's the key to your question. This passion, in my case, comes from the realisation that I found a way of life that is effective and efficient, sustainable and enjoyable. It's as if I woke up from a horrible nightmare of late and over-budget projects, micro-management and wasted time and resources, and it's only logical to defend my new lifestyle with passion. We've been freed and we'll only give up Agile if something better comes up!

That's another reflection of the agilist's argument for agile. We have been living a horrible nightmare, and we see agile as a better dream to dream than the one we've dreamt before. There has been enough positive business outcome from the many experiments we've conducted as a community that we want to keep running experiments and trying the same thing over and over again, with tweaks, to see if we can get it right.

Early in my professional life I had a set of goals, most of which I achieved within the first five years or so. The only goal I couldn't achieve was getting my clients to listen to the users. I saw agile as a way to, among other things, finally reach that goal. And, as my career moved forward to encounter, then exemplify, complexity, the kind of goal setting taught to me in school rarely worked after a certain point in my career. The goals, once achieved, weren't satisfying or meaningful. Things had changed in the meantime. I had changed. Over a period of time, I learned that having an objective and guiding toward it with many tests and explorations was more satisfying and took me more interesting places. Achieving a goal that has lost its luster during pursuit is a hollow thing.

Awakening is Progressive

Though I had come across the poet Theodore Roethke's work as an undergrad and found much of it meaningful, one poem, "The Waking,"[7] has taken on special significance for me and has become, if not a philosophy of life, at least a guiding light. I have been known to plot it on extra-large paper and leave it pinned to my chair as I complete an engagement and leave a work group. It is both a reminder and a comfort and does the job of, keeping us dancing at the edge of the wormhole to a new level of consciousness.

As Jeff Careira says in *Radical Inclusivity: Expanding Our Minds Beyond Dualistic Thinking*, poetry is the best mechanism we have, given our dualistic minds and dualistic language, for upping the odds that we may fortuitously fall through a kind of wormhole between two levels of consciousness. Entering the world of the poem allows us to dance on the edge of such a wormhole so that we might fall through. The kind of change that takes us to the next developmental level is almost always experiential and often, in one way or another, accidental. Poems

Chapter 2: The Agile Journey Is Personal

are pure experience or may be pictures, moments in time, laid out on the page before us. They grab us by the eyes and ears and yank us to another awareness forcing us to notice what was invisible before. This kind of transformative shift is not something we can pursue with structured goal setting but something that we invite in and allow to sneak up on us.

Progressive Awakening

> I wake to sleep, and take my waking slow.
> I feel my fate in what I cannot fear.
> I learn by going where I have to go.
> --Theodore Roethke

This waking—again awakening—
waking again from a sleep
—was I sleeping?
I wake to sleep again:
Perennial awakening.

My fate lies in the work that co-creates me.
I awaken as this being,
dancing from here to there.

In seeing you
I see my Self—just there.
As we relate we co-create the flow.
Emotion's reasoning
helps us to understand and know.

Since I see work as de facto a developmental path and that the social aspects of our work to a large extent forms who we are, I see the waking to sleep and waking again metaphor in the poem above as analogous to the experience of self-discovery we have in the workplace. All of us now are subject to, and participants in, constant change. What we thought we knew to be true about the

Awakening is Progressive

organizations and markets we work in, what our customers want, and what the best way of achieving desired outcomes may be is constantly changing.

"Progressive Awakening" describes for me what agilists welcome as a path of exploration toward the goal of human wholeness. This is also a path toward wholeness in organizations which seek to tune themselves to be profitable enough to support the lives dependent upon them.

Mine

The agile community existed around me before I saw it. My first encounter with agile methods was a presentation on XP, or Extreme Programming, made by Ward Cunningham in the late 90s. The entire team I was working with at the time went together to hear Ward talk. We were the happiest team in the organization, though we were not working on the flagship product. We were led by a hard-working young manager who probably had not been trained for the job of leading or managing. However, he was a natural servant leader, and he had high standards when it came to productivity and quality. As we listened to Ward speak, we were pleased by what he said. We believed we were already doing many of the things he was suggesting to improve teamworking.

Over the following ten years a number of things happened that affected my readiness to invest my time and energy in what the Agile Manifesto and Principles seemed to portend. I moved through a range of roles on software teams. I turned around the most difficult project I've worked on to date, entailing days that started at 6 a.m. and often ran until 9 p.m. while triple-booked during many of the intervening hours. I made the presentation to the Software Process Improvement Network that I described in the introduction to this book. I co-authored a major paper on conflict resolution in software development, of which collaboration is one approach. I created and began teaching a full-day curriculum on

Chapter 2: The Agile Journey Is Personal

collaboration. And, I had the uncommon opportunity of working in an organization that was exploring Scrum, one half of the company using Scrum well and the other half using it deplorably. I sat on the deplorable half, but a manager on the more high-functioning side of the organization invited me to sit in on meetings there. I saw the stark difference in both happiness and productivity.

When I met Norm Kerth, I learned the name of something I had not recognized floating in the software cultural ether all around me. It was called "agile." I wanted to learn more about it and talked to everyone and read everything I could about it. That's how a shift in consciousness can happen. First you don't see things that are all around you; then you do.

It seemed to me that this way of working did, indeed, address the challenges I'd seen in so many of the downsizings and failed projects I'd followed along behind. It seemed to me I had found a way of working that valued a dialogic, collaborative stance that provided a means for individuals to have rich, meaningful lives (at work and at home) while organizations also thrived. My understanding was that, as these organizations targeted lucrative markets, they were constantly learning about those markets while also learning about themselves and their organization's delivery capabilities. This would allow them to make adjustments as they learned.

I hold strong values around the individual's right to self-actualize. I also hold strong values around self-responsibility, and I understand the right to self-actualize in that context. I see every individual's contribution in solving the world's problems as vital, and so, by extension, the agilist's approach to individuals and teams fits well with that. I saw much hope for growing on the job using agile methods and, by extension, making the world a better place.

Mine

My focus has always been on individuals in organizations rather than on organizations themselves. I see that organizations are made up of individuals, and that enlightened individuals in sufficient numbers create enlightened work environments. The social research summarized in books such as *The Corrosion of Character: The Personal Consequences of Work in the New Capitalism* by Richard Sennet and the similar philosophical musings and insights of David Whyte in *The Heart Aroused: Poetry and the Preservation of the Soul in Corporate America* have strongly resonated with the way I see the potential and hazards of the modern organization.

During a night of interrupted sleep in August of 2007, I tuned into an interview of John Rigas by Charlie Rose. The interview was recorded on June 27, 2007, shortly after Rigas and his son Timothy had been convicted of defrauding their shareholders and were ordered to report to prison on August 13, 2007. The interview had taken place at John Rigas' request and the content of that interview exhibited much of what I saw in the more advanced cases of social and ethical disorientation among my colleagues and clients.

My heart went out to Rigas for the effort he was expending in attempting to make sense of his experience and its consequences, particularly during exchanges in which Rose would restate various prosecutorial claims against Rigas and ask him whether he did each of those things. He would admit that he had, then equivocate or try to explain. Then Rose would ask him if he was guilty and Rigas, appearing to my mind like a dismayed Dorian Gray,[§] would answer "They tell me that I am." There is no way that someone in that state of ethical confusion can possibly admit culpability and receive lenience, let alone absolution and forgiveness. Neither can he nor his sympathetic peers learn from his actions: We are all bankrupted by such a state of affairs in organizations. Stories

---

§ Dorian Gray is the protagonist and antihero in Oscar Wilde's novel of manners and morals.

Chapter 2: The Agile Journey Is Personal

like Rigas's are not created overnight, and the organizations that produce them or which they lead are necessarily populated by paler shades of the same color.

Charlie Rose's interview of John Rigas on the cusp of Rigas's and his son's incarceration for defrauding their shareholders was, for me, a potent example of what "playing by the rules" of corporate American had come to mean. Rigas saw himself as having "played by the rules," and as the years have gone by, we have seen many more cases of how playing by such rules have bankrupted us in one way or another.[8] In the face of such examples, we naturally cast about for some means of ensuring our own integrity and of doing what Americans were once known for: pulling ourselves up by our own bootstraps.

At one time, agile frameworks, methods, values, and practices provided a means for doing that: cleaning up the detritus and waste in organizations while improving the character and general lot in life of the individual practitioners.

As blog post after blog post, article after article, and book after book comes out to challenge agile, I see a lot of misunderstanding of agile in general. And, I also see that, for whatever reason, the broader agile community is on a path that looks much like what we once railed against. Some things which brought us to a better way remain. There is still the shelter of each other. There is still the knowledgebase in complexity science, human systems understanding, systems science, organizational dynamics, and product development to draw on. There is much more evidence now to show that we are able to raise our consciousness together in ways that are, essentially, much harder to do alone. And these are the ways most needed in our increasingly urbanized and globalized society.

Mine

What I still value is what brought me to Agile: individuals in organizations pursuing wholeness while fostering a healthy business.

What's Your Attractor?

People come to agile methods, frameworks, principles and practices for many reasons: quality, autonomy, peace of mind, rapid throughput, curiosity—and coolness. The last reason, to my way of thinking, is by far the worst.

As an agile coach, when I am invited into organizations, one of the first questions I ask is "How do you know you need to be agile? Maybe you just need to be lean." The next thing that typically happens is that I am told they are certain they need to be agile. So, then I ask, "How agile do you need to be? How quickly do you need to respond to market changes?" Rarely has the client considered this. However, they are certain they need to use Scrum to get there. And then, because usually I'm talking to people who are building software, we talk about the importance of also adopting technical practices such as pairing, TDD, refactoring, collective code ownership, and so on.

Sometimes, the motivation for "doing Scrum" really is coolness: everyone else is doing it, so we better get on the bandwagon. After all, we need to remain employable. Knowing Scrum is all too often equated with being employable—as opposed to being good at building software supporting employability. The agile movement does have a rock star quality to it, and some of the more well-known consultants have definitely cultivated that "coolness" quality, though coolness has nothing to do with agility. In fact, I am concerned that coolness is a huge distractor from the deep theory and sound principles and practices—and just plain good discipline—that actually results in agility.

Chapter 2: The Agile Journey Is Personal

In a world faced with a lot of problems that always seem to be subdividing and multiplying, agile's experimentation, reflexive thinking, and cross-functional collaboration tenets hold great promise for those who are interested in incremental improvement. However, over the last 15 years, what I've seen happen is the agile community has become more stuck in some ways. We shy away from failure discussions. We let blame and shame not only creep in but flood in. We get chips on our shoulders about our unique "solution" to the puzzle of achieving agility, so we debate and defend rather than inquire and engage in dialogue. We revere rock stars and adulate heroes rather than leveraging our own thinking in the context of community and taking responsibility for making things better where we are.

Your attractor to agile may well be different. Your attractor may be about doing the right thing by the team or finally putting the design of the work back into the hands of the people doing the work. Or, you may be on the path of changing the world as one man I was talking to this morning made clear was his motivation.

Knowing why you prefer to pursue agility even in the face of discouragement and lack of support will help you get through the hard times that agilists often face in the current, transforming world. And, when the deck seems most stacked against you and your advocacy for agility, your self-knowledge will help you understand that even just employing agile tenets in your own life, work, and relationships has value.

Chapter 3: Why Do People Protect Agile?

In April of 2016 I was acting as a facilitator for a subgroup at an annual regional conference on lean and agile sponsored by Intel Corporation. During the conference, Intel announced a market and strategy-driven layoff of historic proportions[9]. Among over 2,000 others, the entire work group that had sponsored that conference was laid off over the next several weeks. It was not the first time I had seen this kind of mass layoff at a large company.

In fact, it sometimes has seemed to me that much of my career has been about coming in after such layoffs and trying to piece together project efforts that were underway before a layoff. In this case, the situation was particularly poignant because, even after the announcement, it appeared that most of the people at this conference continued their focus on the learning rather than throwing up their hands in despair and heading back to the office or home.

These people appeared to care about the community they were experiencing and the learning they were gaining. They persevered in the face of the employment-eliminating effects (for many) of a market that had moved and changed with greater agility than their organization could muster to respond with.

The year before as the result of a much smaller layoff, another former Intel employee had founded a peer support and empowerment group called The Eliminati. They were organized and ready to welcome the new round of "graduates," who came to be known as the "class of 2016." I wrote this poem in an attempt to reflect the grief, shock, and confusion that people in such a situation tend to go through.

The Eliminati

The Eliminati

Something that I was part of,
that I was a part of
but now am apart from . . .
They said "forever"—that it would be forever
if I gave and was loyal,
but this is not forever,
no part of forever that I can identify.

Something I was a part of,
that I am now outside of,
though it is inside me---
in my head; in my heart---
Those friends who left with me,
who did not leave with me,
and so still are a part of
what I am no longer a part of.
That part of me that I left there,
that did not come to this where
is still a part of
what I am no longer a part of.

That piece I miss inside me
that was part of what I was a part of
because they said it would be forever.
This is not forever.
They were clever.
They took that part of me for money
and they didn't give it back.

Agile has spread rapidly not only because it can generate remarkable business results, but when it flourishes in an organization, it helps prevent human experiences like that conveyed in the poem above. The forces that create these unhappy experiences are entrenched in our thinking.

Chapter 3: Why Do People Protect Agile?

Alignment with agile principles and practices helps to move us to new ways of thinking. This helps us unknit the impediments that keep us from delivering the products we need to deliver and getting better together as we need to. Not everyone moves at the same pace in this learning. Those who find the benefits first can be evangelical and even fierce in guarding against the exit of agile practices from their workplaces. They have found a better way of working that results in a better quality of life and, often, puts a higher standard of professional integrity within their grasp.

Who can blame them for seeming a bit ferocious at times?

What is the Ineffable in Agile?

When in April of 2017, I posted that article on LinkedIn[10] , I had noticed a strange phenomenon over the last several years. While ideal agile adoptions were scarce and failure stories were thick on the ground, the participants in agile projects often referred to agile as something better than the approaches they had routinely experienced in the past.

In fact, for years, when I'd be coaching a team that was complaining about the process changes that come with moving to agile methods I'd say, "Okay, fine. Maybe we're attempting to change too quickly. Would you like to go back? We can go back any time you like." I've never had a team vote to leave agile methods behind. There may be a strong naysayer or two, but the team tends to help them see the value in agile methods or to move them along and give the process another chance.

The quotes from LinkedIn members at the beginning of this chapter show that I am among many when I say that people reach out for something ineffable, transformative, or transcendental, when they reach out for agile. This is also true of my many conversations with people in the companies in which I have consulted, in the agile community where I am an active participant,

What is the Ineffable in Agile?

and with the agile coaches across the US and around the world with whom I've been having this conversation lately.

Many people are reaching out for business results when they turn to agile practices, but many at various levels in the organization are reaching out for more than that. Their expressed desires are for a better world through a better way of working. Whether they put their hopes in getting to that better world through technical practices, through data-driven methods of right-sizing work to capacity to prevent exhaustion of workers, through deep dialogue on teams, or through faster throughput of higher quality products and services, they have hope for a better state of things. And, these hopes are not always realized through agile, particularly when agile frameworks are implemented as work process management systems.

Many people understand that the way we spend our days, the work we do and how we do it, does much to make us the people that we are. Knowledge workers in particular are made in and through their work, and their products are often artifacts of self-expression. Many of the senior, more experienced programmers I've worked with have philosophies of craft that underscore the importance of quality in their work and give particular attention to their needs for autonomy in practicing their craft. My own experience is that my career has had a tremendous influence on who I am.

David Whyte is a consulting corporate poet with a client list that eventually included such American giants as Shell Oil. In 1994, he published The Heart Aroused: Poetry And The Preservation Of The Soul In Corporate America. Whyte evokes the experience of the worker in a complex organization and how his existence in that organization affects his character over time.

He describes the corporation as a larger body that, essentially, makes it possible for the individual to achieve what is not

Chapter 3: Why Do People Protect Agile?

achievable as an individual; yet, the corporation also renders the individual powerless. He likens the organization to an engulfing parent which, by both encouraging creativity and limiting it, creates a tremendous pressure in the individual that eventually leads to the individual caving in to the system or leaving in anger to find a place where the individual's true work can be done[11] .

For some people, this is what retirement looks like. For others, "retiring on the job" is an alternative to consciously experiencing the onslaughts against their character.

Over time, and perhaps as an aspect of the "caving in" described above, enduring this kind of tension in one's work life engenders "an almost pleasurable gleam of wickedness, that we have earned some kind of right through our blood and sweat to have less interest. We look but do not care to perceive[12] . . ." Whyte's analogy of the malaise of the individual worker stepping over some sort of obstruction in the doorway to the workplace each day and then one day realizing that obstruction is a corpse and that corpse is her own is apt. As Whyte says "We flee . . . The grief is too much[13].

Whyte describes the effects of compromise of the self on the job. His metaphorical approach is all too resonant for many of us, and to defend against it becoming our story, we reach out to the ineffable in agile as a bulwark against that dark time. We reach out to it for ourselves, our colleagues, and our organizations.

What Do We Think We're Protecting?

The agile movement has its roots in lean and in work process and organizational development experiments done on many projects in the software development industry in the late 1990s and formalized through the publication of the Agile Manifesto in 2001. Whatever becomes of agile, its effects will

What Do We Think We're Protecting?

remain, if nothing else, as a romantic influence in the software development industry.

Some people might find this notion of a neo-romantic movement in software development amusing. And, yes, I'm referring to the same kind of romantic movement that started in Europe among the core creatives—writers, artists, poets, philosophers and musicians—in the late 18th century.

The romantic movement of the 18th century emphasized emotion and the individual in a reaction to the mechanization of the industrial revolution, the social and political dynamics of the enlightenment, and other aspects of modernity such as the scientific rationalization and decomposition of nature. The agile movement has emphasized human experience in the context of intellectually demanding work. It has touted scientific explanations of alternative methods of organizing work and relating to people. Agile practices act to restructure the classist power dynamics of bureaucratic, hierarchical, power-over management structures. It endorses redistributing power to line workers and instituting experiment-driven and flow-based models of developing products and services.

The agilists have made their point and had their effect. The American Management Association[¶] recognizes the value of agile methods as does the Project Management Institute[**] and the US federal government.[††] The Harvard Business Review online

---

[¶] The American Management Association offers seminars on agile.
http://www.amanet.org/site-search-results.aspx?search_terms=Agile
[**] The February 2017 edition of the PMI Pulse of the Profession points to agile as a key reason that project success rates have increased after several years of stagnation. https://www.pmi.org/learning/thought-leadership/pulse/pulse-of-the-profession-2017
[††] U.S. CIO Urges Feds to Fail Fast, Not Fail Big
http://www.cio.com/article/2378864/government-use-of-it/u-s--cio-urges-feds-to-fail-fast--not-fail-big.html

Chapter 3: Why Do People Protect Agile?

knowledgebase, when searched for the term "agile," returns over a thousand results, many of the top-ranked hits authored or co-authored by well-known names in the agile movement. And, increasingly, in late 2016 and 2017, that well-respected journal has published articles implicitly focused on management methods that align with the Agile Manifesto and Principles.

We seem to be in the later stages of an historical evolution wherein we have moved from a nomadic tribal existence in early human history; to an agricultural clan-based society; to the founding of monarchies; the deposing of monarchies in favor of democracy, socialism, and communism; moving toward a deeply democratic global community currently struggling with the effects of class-based economic disparity and authoritarianism. Overall, the thrust appears to be in favor of the individual's value and salience in the context of the community. It should give us pause to note that, when each of the types of governance I've just cited was in practice, people—individuals and groups—acted to cause the evolution of governance. In each case, at the global level, we have reached out for more individual freedom and struggled to grapple effectively with individual accountability. As we progressively meet our needs according to Maslow's Hierarchy[‡‡] self-determination becomes more important.

The agile movement is another expression of such an attempt. When we protect agile we are protecting our right to self-actualization and self-determination without threat of real or symbolic death (work dislocation). At the same time, as part of a system, we have certain accountabilities to others, and we have been challenged about how to meet those accountabilities.

Knowledge workers, especially computer programmers, are sufficiently well-compensated to have met their lower level

---

‡‡ http://psychclassics.yorku.ca/Maslow/motivation.htm retrieved 8/13/17

What Do We Think We're Protecting?

needs thereby putting pressure on them to satisfy their higher-level needs.

As members of the creative class their desires for exploration, self-expression, and control over their work can be significant.

The nature of the industry when agile methods emerged was such that small groups could develop and experiment with practices that could be re-used in larger organizational groups. Many experiments could be run without having to restructure organizations. For example, some years ago on a state government project in trouble, I ran two experiments: one in which we delivered a series of reports iteratively and staged them in a testing area accessible to the customer to facilitated customer testing and one in which we evolved a product owner type role that was responsible for business requirements development and approval. These experiments were such a success that the project was delivered just slightly ahead of schedule. These two experiments were run locally in a project that was surrounded by the ultimate example of bureaucracy: government.

Software organizations are founded and evolve in such a way that, as methods develop inside teams, organizational practices can evolve experimentally in small organizations. Large organizations can run experiments in subgroups within them. The difficulty of running work process experiments increases with the level of integration of the bureaucracy and the depth of the hierarchy. Pain and ongoing disappointment tend to ensue in such cases.

Meanwhile, those teams that had been successful in their experiments and could replicate them and codify them as methods or frameworks that both benefit the self-efficacy of teams and the profitability of products—those teams and organizations were very happy with agile methods. The desire for self-determination on the part of teams and team members could be gratified. Cases were shared formally and anecdotally until even the largest

Chapter 3: Why Do People Protect Agile?

organizations in the world, faced with continuing volatility, uncertainty, complexity, and ambiguity, wanted in on the action.

Agile exploded across business domains.

As one Certified Scrum Trainer said to me a few years ago, "Everyone's doing agile, but really, no one is doing agile." We're well aware of the "daily standup as agility marker" phenomenon. We don't need to spend time on it here.

So, while we reach out for greater self-determination, self-actualization, and self-efficacy for ourselves and the individuals in the organizations we care about, the reality is that agile methods are adopted more often as work process management systems than organizational transformation methods. And, here is where things begin to break down and heartbreak can ensue.

Chapter 4: The Agile Affect

Several years ago, I was coaching a Scrum Master who had been assigned to the role without being trained first. He was struggling with how to perform as a Scrum Master. He was used to being a functional manager with direct reports. One day he said to me, "I get it now. The difference between being a manager and being a Scrum Master is mostly about affect." I had to think about that for a while. I wondered where he had gotten that idea. He was in most of the same coaching conversations as the other two Scrum Masters in his group. Finally, we sat down and had a conversation about his belief system around people, and I realized that he believed that "showing them the whip" was ultimately required in many cases to get people to perform. And, it almost seemed that this belief on his part created the related response from the team he was supposed to be serving. They had fretful planning days, had a hard time getting along, and they regularly failed to deliver while he stood back and observed, despaired, and prepared to show them the whip.

Agile is not just about affect, but affect matters. "Affect" has to do with the apparent and expressed emotion in our presence. The nature of a skilled agilist's presence is often more receptive and facilitative than that of people who are not steeped in the values, principles, and cultural precepts of the agile community. Such people value integrating and sharing power with those they lead or work with. It is incumbent on them to self-manage, especially, their emotional state because they are aware of the human system they are influencing.

The first of the values in the Agile Manifesto is "Individuals and interactions over processes and tools," and this has much to do with the social environment in agile-aspiring organizations. A key learning that is applied every day is that the human system, the work system, and the product are all entangled with each other.

Does Shielding Always Help?

We find that preventing unnecessary and unhelpful stress, tension, and fear in the environment helps people focus and work together.

Does Shielding Always Help?

Many of us feel that shielding people from unnecessary negative emotion is a sign of respect: we're not flogging them anymore. We recognize their connectedness as a work group and how that connectedness benefits them, the work, and society at large. And, we recognize their connectedness with us, which motivates us even more to see to their needs, for in so doing, we see to our own.

This means that agilists are often concerned about the emotional tenor and intensity of conversations, work groups, and organizations. They care about tools and approaches to self-management that support connectedness.

In agile-aspiring teams and organizations, we are often looking at the entanglement of the worker with the work and the work with the customer. We are trying to determine where to make adjustments to improve work life quality, product quality, and throughput. We apply "hard skills," such as code quality analysis and continuous delivery. And, we apply "soft skills," in conversations of various sorts such as retrospectives and planning events. Both the appropriate application of hard skills and soft skills is required, and certainly it's with the soft skills that affect is important. However, affect is not everything, as the Scrum Master I cited above surmised.

What has become debatable in my mind is the extent to which the hard skills are not related to the soft skills and to the ineffable in agile. What non-technologists think of as hard skills are, to the worker adept at using those skills, as natural as conversation.
The key point in *Technical Practices as a Hack on Consciousness: Why to Hack Yourself*,[14] was that technical practices which are dialogic in nature, though hard skills, have an unappreciated value

in actualizing the ineffable in agile. In fact, a heightened state of consciousness in the workplace is what many of us are pursuing through our work as agilists—every bit as much as profit through better quality products delivered in a timely fashion.

We know something is wrong in the world of work. Our instincts, the quantum theory, and our experiments in our own lives say that some of this wrongness we can fix through how we treat each other as we organize work to deliver complex solutions to complex problems. As we learn about quantum theory—those learnings in physics, biology, and mathematics that help us see the flaws in the Newtonian model of the world—we understand more and more what our intuition is picking up. We are conscious quantum beings trying to function in mechanistic Newtonian structures to do knowledge work. Agile may currently only contain a set of transitional processes that help us along on the path to more skillfully attaining that heightened state of consciousness in and at work. But they are the best we've had to date.

Transitional Object ←→ Transitional Methods

Some people say that the vocabulary, the events, the principles and practices we use in pursuing agility amount to a religion. That's not a very comfortable notion for many of us. We like to think we're more scientific in our approach than that.

Recently, someone outside the agile community highlighted the notion of transitional objects and transitional processes to me. The most common notion of a transitional object are artifacts, such as icons, statues, chalices, and clothing, used during rituals that draw us closer to what we identify as god. He also talked about the notion of a transitional process, such as focusing on a stone while relaxing the mind as a practice, or transitional process, for attaining greater mindfulness. He referred to these objects and practices as interim steps when the "next step is too big." My teacher in this case is a bodyworker, dancer, and golfer who works with athletes and dancers who are pursuing next steps that are sometimes too big—so they end up on his massage table.

I see Scrum, Extreme Programming, Kanban and their attendant practices as transitional practices that are the best we have—for now—as we pursue the ineffable in agile. The ineffable in agile is related to the simultaneous importance and value of the individual (the node) and the value of the connections between all individuals (the network). The attainment of self-transcendence is what our relatively inept conversations around servant leadership and egoless programming point to. As I asserted to my co-author of "Technical Practices as a Hack on Consciousness: Why to Hack Yourself," it takes a strong ego to be an egoless programmer.

What has attracted many of us to agile is not only its promise for better quality software more appropriately tuned for its market and created in more humane environments. Many of us also saw the larger system transformation that seemed possible through the values and principles in the manifesto and its supporting principles.

Apparently with this hope in view, agile has been embroidered with much that the original creators and signers of the manifesto likely never imagined. The work of a broad range of other thinkers, from Virginia Satir, to Daniel Pink, to Ralph Kilmann and Kenneth Thomas, to Margaret Wheatley and Peter Senge, to Otto Scharmer, to Erwin Schroedinger is commonly cited in conversation among agilists. Actually, the list is nearly endless because it is constantly expanding as thinking agilists everywhere pursue a greater grasp of all that helps the team or organization they serve to be agile. And sometimes, agilists also look hard at what helps *them* be agile.

Agile transformations are always ultimately personal. But, we have not seen that or behaved as if it were so. We have behaved as if it were a systems problem "out there" all too often rather

Chapter 4: The Agile Affect

than seeing that there is also a necessity for transformation "in here."

The Best that Agile Offers

In the best agile adoptions, failure is recognized, accepted, and mined for learning. The team feels supported, and the business's needs are met. The workers evolve together. Conflict is engaged productively for its creative and consciousness-raising value as well as necessity in solving problems to move the work forward. Workers at all levels of the organization learn about themselves and each other, become more aware of their context, and start noticing valuable information they might previously have discounted as unimportant.

Following are some descriptions of teams that exemplify what agile can do for human effort and human being.

A Team Turnaround in Government

One of the first agile teams I coached sticks in my mind as a fine example of how agile practices can improve the lot of human beings and their collective effort. This team was in a government agency with a state-level mandate to create a new data system that interfaced between the Department of Human Services and the State Police's driver's license database to regulate the granting and maintenance of an ID card that gave access to alternative healthcare.

By the time I joined the effort, there had been forty-seven people through the seven seats on the team, eight project managers, five architectures, and three years lost and three million dollars spent. Meanwhile, nothing had been delivered. The customer, as you might imagine, was not happy. The project had a citizen oversight committee that drew up as many as or more than fifty attendees and three sets of television cameras to their meetings. The management team wasn't just on the hot seat, it was frying.

And things weren't so great for the application development team, either. Every time things started to go south on the project, managers would blame the team. Generally, some or all of the team lost their jobs. Sometimes they'd decide the architecture was the problem, so they'd re-architect. But, in three years, they never delivered anything.

Meanwhile, the database for the existing application was so unstable that it would lock up multiple times per day. Whenever that happened, the eighteen data entry operators who were taking the place of the automated system still in development had to exit the system immediately. The system had to be restarted, and they never knew if this was going to be the time when the database wouldn't come back—and thousands upon thousands of records would be lost. At least they'd have the hardcopy versions: The program was receiving such high usage that eighteen data entry operators couldn't keep up. There were rolling walls of hard copy files waiting to be entered.

The software development team wasn't doing much better. They were in despair. They didn't have the tools they needed. They had no respect from the management team. They were drowning, not swimming.

The simple agile principle of delivering early and often gave us an easy win. They had had a partially working version of the front page of the web app ready for months. Previously, they had been prevented from delivering it because it looked incomplete, and therefore unacceptable to them. The team set up their first demo to get feedback on what they had so far, and showed the customer what we had. It was as though we had been hiding a treasure. The customer was delighted!

Chapter 4: The Agile Affect

The customer was so encouraged that they were willing to dedicate the manager of the data entry team to the project as the Product Owner. Then, we got to work largely revising the existing backlog so that the team had stories they could work on. The team rapidly regained their sense of meaning, and as they regained their sense of pride, by delivering sprint-over-sprint, usually to the satisfaction of the Product Owner and the stakeholders she brought with her to the Sprint Review, their whole sense of themselves as a team blossomed. After three years of non-delivery, they delivered the application in in less than a year. The executive sponsor was so energized by the agile approach we were using, he delayed his retirement and increased his engagement in the project.

A Team with Heart, Music, and Dogs

The next team that comes to mind is a more recent example. When I joined the effort, the team was supposedly using agile methods, Scrum specifically. My first day with them was a day-long immersion interview. I watched while the technical lead berated the team, and some individuals, mercilessly. They had just hired a trained and experienced Scrum Master, and their Product Owner was in the process of leaving. The backlog was a stack of defects. The team had been sequestered on site with the co-development partner by their customer because their delivery reliability had been so poor. The customer's response was to monitor and task them at a lower and lower level.

This, of course, wasn't working.

In short order, and to the relief of everyone but his manager, the berating technical lead resigned. We talked among ourselves and the team decided they wanted to take their destiny back into their own hands.

The Best that Agile Offers

The team decided to build a fort to keep themselves safe in the face of a tremendously challenging project:

- Focus
- Openness
- Respect
- Trust

Their FORT would be their protection as they started their recovery.

Together we looked at our inability to generate testable builds, and applauded ourselves for the great team dynamics we had even in the face of the ill treatment and disrespect we had experienced. After proving we could deliver and did care about the customer's integration deadlines, we escaped from the client site where we had been housed under very uncomfortable conditions and returned to our own offices where the team could have their dogs and their music, and where they could speak freely.

I remember being impressed with the team's eagerness to learn. Their Scrum Master was dedicated to teaching them "Scrum by the book," so they could get a taste of that before they started embroidering it with what they *thought* Scrum was. A new Technical Product Owner was hired, and the true state of the backlog was made clear, as was the state of the skills on the team. The team was under-skilled for the challenge in front of them.

The team was eager to learn, so management negotiated with their business partner to loan us their technical practices coach. One day of technical practices coaching had a lightning rod effect on the team. Suddenly they realized more about where they were in comparison with where they wanted to be. This both sobered and excited them. Then they started working together more closely and working more strategically. They wanted to understand how cross-functional communication could bring them a bigger payoff. They learned about Pervasive Leadership, a leadership model I had created (see Appendix A), which introduced them to their own value as leaders and the imperative of their assuming leadership. And, they took ownership of the project.

Impediments that would have stopped them in their tracks previously, such as running out of tasks or difficulties in scheduling, were easily moved by the team themselves. When things went wrong, such as a broken build, they called for help from other team members and went to work on the problem, whereas before, they would have wasted cycles in unproductive fretting rather than productive problem solving. Management stood back in frank surprise.

Everyone learned that there are technical practices in Extreme Programming that are vital to keeping a Scrum Team building good software. Everyone learned about Pervasive Leadership, which woke them up to their own power and responsibility to lead. In a matter of days, they were solving problems, helping each other, focused on the customer, and beginning to understand how to lead the project as well or better than the managers they were looking to for leadership in all things previously.

For example, the relationship between the team's organization and their business partner's organization was very rough. This was affecting interorganizational team dynamics and wasting time in getting the work done. The team could see this for themselves and raised a number of things they wished they had done sooner, for instance, integrating the two organizations' teams for troubleshooting.

The team reached out directly to their colleagues at the team level in the partner organization and invited them to come onsite on an as-needed basis where they could work as an integrated team in a dedicated team room. The team made the decision to do this and did almost all of the negotiation themselves as well as scheduling the visits. They only escalated when managers on the business partner's organization blocked their requests, which they did, at first. As part of this co-working arrangement, the team worked hard to repair the relationship between the two companies while appropriately retaining confidentiality for their employer.

The Teams that were Coached Backwards

Another group of three teams had developed an increasing pattern of failing over a three-year period. They were working on re-coding and enhancing their already successful flagship product on another technical stack. They were "using Scrum," and had been coached by someone who "taught us the philosophy and then told us to go figure it out." The company had shrunk fifty percent through voluntary and involuntary terminations during the time they were "doing Scrum" based on this person's coaching. The pattern of forcing work into the team had become so routine that, when I led the first thorough retrospective some team members were shocked to learn that they were supposed to understand the work they were taking in before they committed to it.

I suggested everyone read the Agile Manifesto and Principles and that at least the Scrum Masters, but preferably everyone, read the Scrum Guide. They learned that they were missing a role and the entire review meeting as well as most of the intent of the retrospective. They learned that there was such a thing as Scrum Theory. They learned that there were strategies and tactics for turning around a failing sprint; they didn't have to just submit to imminent failure and disappointment again.

They decided to make some big changes, and we started inserting targeted learning and coaching opportunities into their sprints and looking for opportunities to bring learning from the

Chapter 4: The Agile Affect

last sprint into the current sprint. The management team learned that, while the team is the engine of the organization, the heart that pumps the blood, the management team is the shadow heart that pumps the lymph fluid through the body of the organization and keeps the immune system in good order so the team can thrive as it pursues agility.

But, it doesn't always go that way.

The Dark Side of Agile

When in 2006 I read Ken Schwaber's "Scrum Musings," a collection of essays that predated his books, it seemed to me that what was being described was simply good project management. As I learned more about Scrum and Extreme Programming, I became aware of the deep theory around human systems, digital systems design, and business management that were ingeniously simplified in these approaches. Over the years, I've learned that most of what is taught as Scrum, XP, and Kanban have been around many years, even for generations. One person cited the roots of the pairing practice as originating in the 1950s. What seems to be freshest in agile is the *packaging* and the *socioeconomic environment* in which agile has surfaced.

The Agile Manifesto and Principles emerged at the same time that more linear and, often, power-over, even authoritarian, approaches to software development were being codified in software development. I have my own memories of catching a nap under my desk so I could keep working, thirteen hour shifts with a fifteen-minute break, and software I'd spent months working on being delivered to market with marketing materials that touted features it didn't have. Some managers I come across today still believe that a "pep talk" is all that exhausted and confused software teams need in order to go that last mile at top speed toward an ever-receding shippable product. The packaging of agile has in some cases now overwhelmed the content of its message, with

The Dark Side of Agile

high-voltage conferences and rock star consultants and speakers dominating the stage. This can draw one kind of audience while, of course, repelling another.

Two years ago, I was asked to co-present with a colleague who comes more from the traditional side of the business philosophical spectrum. Many times, he'd raised a question about what was so different about agile and what was it that agilists felt they were protecting? Why did they seem so defensive when their cute terms and ways of doing things
were questioned?

I told him that it seemed to me that many of these people had experienced or witnessed *real harm* at the hands of managers thinking in the traditional paradigm in the past. They have found something that works for them, and they are very concerned about it being taken away and the work environment returning to how they had been. He was thoughtful about this, and we ended up having many conversations about whether managers coming from a traditional paradigm could be true servant leaders. We talked about what the effect of a power-over[§§] approach to leading people tended to be with knowledge workers (especially software developers) and also about the importance and value of acknowledging that some of the roots of agile were in traditional management thinking, which itself had gone awry in application.

We ended up creating a presentation about our thinking and delivering it together in June of 2014. It included a list of fifty-eight agile practices identified by the Agile Alliance, most of which traditionalists would recognize.

---

§§ Power-over and power-with are two ways of describing how power relationships work. Power-over relationships or leadership stances tend to be more autocratic in nature, while power-with relationships or leadership stances are more cooperative and egalitarian in nature.

Chapter 4: The Agile Affect

The dark side of agile is that many of the frameworks and practices make a very effective bludgeon, especially if they are implemented using a forcing factor or as a work process management tool rather than a cultural evolution method.

Additionally, sometimes the person or people who are driving the agile adoption have had a long and unresolved history of abuse at the hands of traditional methods, and this translates unhelpfully into the way they introduce agile into their environment. They may come across as pitying the victims they see all around them, crusading against the surrounding system, or even as having a chip on their shoulders that makes it difficult for them to have productive conversations with non-aligned stakeholders in the emergence of agile.

The conversation between agilists and traditionalists remains a difficult one. Perhaps that is because everyone, whether they identify with the agile or the traditional community, is still transitioning to this new way of seeing and being in the world of which the agile movement is a forerunner in the business community. Some are jealous of the journey and want to be seen as leaders on the path. Others dislike the nature of the trek or believe they arrived long ago. Yet, it seems that, on this path, no one has truly arrived. In its fullest sense, it's about more than team or organizational agility.

I discussed the potential of software's ability to move the world elsewhere in that article.[15] At approximately the same time my co-author and I were bringing our article on consciousness hacking through the use of certain technical practices, Mikey Siegel was negotiating and facilitating a discussion between Ken Wilber and his approximately year old consciousness hacking organization[¶¶] in Palo Alto, which has since spread around the world. This community is interested in evolving a new human operating system for the planet, a goal which, arguably, agile can help

¶¶ https://www.infoq.com/articles/technical-hack-conciousness

achieve through enlightened software development. The premise of that organization is that, while technology has not done as much as it could to deliver happiness and heighten consciousness, there is much it can do, and we should investigate and experiment with its potential.

Co-hackers worldwide are exploring cyber and socio-technical methods to explore consciousness and create products and experiences to heighten consciousness to support humanity in, as Ken Wilber exhorted them in July of 2017,[16] waking up and growing up. Their slogan is to create a new human operating system for the planet. This is a notion whose time has come.

We can also use a new human operating system for business. I wrote this poem to capture the spirit of the traditional versus agile advocacy conversation, though it's less rancorous than many such conversations I've been a party to.

We Dance

Coming together for sustenance and connection
adapting to our context, eye-gliding as we flow.
We unfold in mutual contribution and connection.

Shall we Gantt this twisting, turning gallivant?
Measure this music? Dance only until the tune stops?
We come together for sustenance and connection!

Is each dance an effort or
a spinning, stepping exploration of our connection?
We unfold in mutual contribution and connection.

Each pair of dancers teams, projects a new pattern
on the floor, stepping in the line of dance
as they come together for sustenance and connection.

Chapter 4: The Agile Affect

Strong leads, strong follows trade lead and follow
as hips sway, arms raise, and backs bend.
We unfold in mutual contribution and creation.

Which way to lead or follow? Which dance is best?
Depends on the music. I prefer a strong connection.
Coming together for sustenance and connection,
we unfold in mutual contribution and creation.

The dark side of agile adoptions that have gone wrong has attracted a lot of attention in the last several years. Agile methods do not always save the day, nor can they.

I remember being called in to chat with a process quality assurance consultant whose job it was to provide project process quality and governance feedback on an extremely public and important state government healthcare project some years ago. The project had been running for nearly two years and was a week out from a big bang delivery. Everything was broken: human systems, work processes, status reporting, and the software. The QA consultant said that, since this was an agile effort, he wanted to know what could be done to turn around the situation at this point. I said, "Nothing." There was no way to save or turn around a project of that magnitude in that condition within a week. Agile is not magic.

The various lawsuits, public scandals, and organizational retrenchments that occurred thereafter went on for years.
The entire effort had been a waste, and there was no possible recovery.

Some people would say that the people "using agile" or "doing agile" on that project were not actually adhering to the values in the manifesto or doing the work according to its supporting principles. And, they'd probably be right. In fact, I know enough about that organization prior to that big, famous, failed project to know it was extremely likely that they'd be right. That doesn't mitigate the fact that it was known as an "agile" effort, and it failed famously.

What the Data Highlights

While agile approaches to organizing work and working with people can have profoundly positive outcomes, many agile adoptions are only nominally agile. Agility is more than affect, though a friendly, egalitarian, and facilitative affect can be helpful. Agility comes about through a focus on people, but it also does not come about through coddling people.

There are a few annual surveys and analytical reports that evaluate the state of agile. The most often referenced one is called The State of Agile Development Survey.[17] It is sponsored by VersionOne™, an agile lifecycle management tool vendor. VersionOne™ contracts with a third party to do the research and write the report, so there is some degree of arms-length evaluation. It should be noted that, every year, I hear experienced agilists raise questions about what the data reported in this survey actually means. Any survey can be questioned, and perhaps VersionOne™ does not describe its methods or approach well enough and does not put enough context around the numbers it is reporting. However, this is the best survey we have to date, and many people make decisions based on this data each year—and have for the eleven preceding years. So, it seems that the community and businesses interested in pursuing agility find some value in it. Otherwise, I surmise, an alternative competing report would be as well-known and referenced.

The following tables are based on data presented in that report regarding the challenges responding organizations found when trying to implement agile and how they measure success. In all three tables, respondents were allowed to indicate more than one choice in response to the question. Note the items I've bolded.

Chapter 4: The Agile Affect

Nature of Challenge	%Effected
Company philosophy or culture at odds with core agile values	**63%**
Lack of experience with agile methods	47%
Lack of management support	**45%**
General organization resistance to change	**43%**
Lack of business/customer/product owner	41%
Insufficient training	34%
Pervasiveness of traditional development	**34%**
Inconsistent agile practices and process	31%
Fragmented tooling, data, and measurements	20%
Ineffective collaboration	**19%**
Regulatory compliance and governance	15%
Don't know	2%

Table 1: Challenges Experienced While Adopting and Scaling Agile[18]

All of the bolded items above indicate a collective consciousness misaligned with the pursuit of agility.

Organizations are comprised of people. And, though organizational processes, espoused philosophies, and culture form and inform the nature of the people who work there, it is people who created and adhere to the processes, philosophies, and culture. They were not created outside of the grasp of human control. Organizations choose people who will have an easier adjustment to the kind of compliance that organization seeks. This represents the nature of the consciousness they choose to maintain. And organizations tend to reward compliance with this kind of consciousness. It is difficult to get rewards for non-compliance. As Seth Godin points out in his talk "Stop Stealing Dreams,"[19] American school systems are designed to create workers who will comply with the kind of industrial thinking that built these organizations. So, it's predictable that when a model of thinking comes along that flies in the face of

What the Data Highlights

industrial, mechanistic thinking that the organization itself will block change.

To be clear, virtually all of the factors cited in the table above point to a consciousness at odds with, not just change, and certainly not just agile values, principles, and practices, but with an unfamiliar and unlike consciousness. The items bolded in Table 1 indicate an organizational consciousness that is aware of and chooses to notice different things than is useful for agility. How that organizational consciousness understands itself and the others it is related to and dependent upon is not in alignment with the values expressed in the Agile Manifesto.

The following two tables are also based on data reported in the The State of Agile Development Survey. The topic of failure is complex. On any given project team of seven, for example, people may disagree about whether a failure has occurred. Though the organizational definition of success may say the project or initiative was a success, three people may agree with that assessment and four people may feel it was a failure. Success is at least as complex a topic. The two tables on the following page describe how organizations included in this survey evaluate success.

Chapter 4: The Agile Affect

Success Criteria	Valued by
On-time delivery	53%
Business value	46%
Customer/user satisfaction	44%
Product quality	42%
Product scope	40%
Productivity	25%
Project visibility	25%
Predictability	23%
Process improvement	21%
Don't know	11%

Table 2: Success of Agile Initiatives[20]
Based on the top five criteria in each table:

Agile initiatives are considered successful when they are delivered on time, provide expected business value, please customers, have sufficient quality and deliver expected scope.

Agile projects are considered successful when they are delivered on time when they have a high rate of throughput of work, show the rate at which they are pushing work through.

Success Criteria	Valued by
Velocity	67%
Iteration burndown	51%
Release burndown	38%
Planned vs. actual stories per iteration	37%
Burn-up chart	34%
Work-in-Process (WIP)	32%
Defects into production	30%
Customer/user satisfaction	28%
Planned vs. actual release dates	26%
Cycle time	23%
Defects over time	23%
Business value delivered	23%
Budget vs. actual cost	22%
Defect resolution	20%
Cumulative flow chart	19%
Test pass/fail over time	16%
Scope change in a release	16%
Estimation accuracy	15%
Individual hours per iteration/week	15%
Earned value	8%
Product utilization	7%
Revenue/sales impact	7%
Customer retention	7%

Table 3: Success of Agile Projects[21]

The success metrics shown in the tables above are metrics that meet the needs of the organization in ways that are not likely to evolve the consciousness of the organization unless the initiative planners and project leaders employ radically different planning and leadership approaches. The qualitative experience of agile methods for *individuals* in the organization can leave some agile champions who entered the field on behalf of human thriving feeling a sense of failure. Measures of human thriving are missing from the success criteria valued by agile-aspiring organizations, though (apparently improved) team morale is cited by 31%[22] of the organizations responding to the survey as a reason for adopting agile and by 81%[23] as a benefit of adopting agile.

Agile adoptions that focus only or primarily on the generation of business value or rapidity of throughput risk not evolving beyond a mechanistic consciousness. The cost of this tends to be blunted agility and arguably a fragile, time-limited agile adoption. Though agile methods have entered the awareness of mainstream business, as the 11th Annual State of Agile Report,[24] articles in the Harvard Business Review, and emergence of separate areas of focus in organizations such as Cutter, Accenture, and Gartner have demonstrated, to many the focus seems to have slipped a bit. Some would argue that we have moved away somewhat from the focus on the individuals and leaned more in the direction of the organizational economic system and consciousness that it is grounded in.

In the tables shown above, we get a sense, based on what's being measured, which many agilists would identify as classic organizational impediments to agility, that the human system is seen as a kind of machine with outputs related to productivity and reliability that we can measure. And, speed and quality with regard to meeting market needs are the highest values as opposed to human learning and development and the human experience of work life, which can be as effective in delivering these desired outcomes.

So, What Were We Meaning To Do?

In a video titled, "The History of the Agile Movement,"[25] Ken Schwaber, co-creator of the Scrum framework, provides some insight into what led up to the development and signing of the Agile Manifesto. He talks about the fact that there is a myth that agile sprang forth fully formed in 2001. "Agile comes out of many ideas and much thinking that has been done in software development and development in general and lean manufacturing that has been done over the last 20 or 30 years."

The urgency that drove the experiments that led to the publication of the manifesto had much to do with organizations trying to survive. He says, "We are probably one of the few industries where our customers can't wait to get rid of us." He goes on to cite one large company that figured its projects typically cost $1.2M if the work was kept onshore. If they took the work offshore, each failed project would only cost them $300K. They were looking, not at going offshore so they had teams that were better at software development, but on saving cost on failure. The cost of employing teams offshore was significantly cheaper, so when the inevitable failures occurred, the decreased staff cost would result in cheaper cost of failure.

Many people saw transformational possibilities in agile, but this video emphasizes the business focus. Resonant conversations coincidentally occurring among many theorists in many fields were gradually drawn into the agile movement. These conversations had much to do the with the human experience of work.

As time has passed, while the agile movement struggled into the awareness of traditional business, the urgency for greater human capability in the face of a VUCA world has increased its pressure upon us all. The increasing incidence of agile adoptions focused on work processes as opposed to human development showers upon us stories of painful human experiences and more and more public claim of the failure of agile to "deliver." Those who came to agile for the human potential expansion it seemed to offer either stand their ground and fight with the same

What the Data Highlights

old tools, become despairing and depart, or, sometimes, become embittered.

In 2014 a group demographically similar to that which created the Agile Manifesto and Principles created the Responsive Manifesto. Responsive strikes an even bolder claim for the human spirit. While the conversation in the agile movement remains focused on "learning," voices in the Responsive movement speak of "development" and raise concerns about focusing on "learning." (See Appendix B for further discussion.) Why might they want to focus on development rather than learning? Because learning can keep us stuck getting better and better at being in our current stage of development and pull resources from evolving to the next possible stage of development.

Chapter 5: Consciousness Not Mindset

Had the agile movement truly clasped hands with the human potential movement, we might be experiencing a different outcome. People from many domains—philosophy, theology, physics, biology, cosmology, and medicine to name a few, have been studying human consciousness for generations. Consciousness theorists have mapped the development of human consciousness in phases across time and aligned it with human development. Through most of the 20th century we only had maps of child development, and there was a culturally implied assumption that, once you reached your age of majority—18, 21, or 25—your development was complete. You might learn new skills such as playing the piano, coding a software language, or the rules of etiquette for a new community, for instance, but you wouldn't truly develop, or increase in internal complexity, as a child does as she grows and develops.

Discovery of "Mindset"

Instead, the agile movement discovered the very valuable notion of mindset. I see this as too mechanistic and temporary to help us bridge to the next level of development necessary for true agility. To truly transform as individuals and thereby be effective constituents in a transformed or transforming organization we need to focus on developing an agile consciousness. A mindset can be adopted while we're working on an agile project and then cast aside when the next project is not agile in its approach. It can be adopted while in the office and cast off during our commute home. Each time we set that mindset aside and practice a non-agile mindset, we risk losing competency in the agile mindset, and lose opportunities to deepen and strengthen that mindset. We take off the "glasses" through which we were viewing the world and miss opportunities to support the transformation of other systems by being agile members of that system.

Discovery of "Mindset"

Evolving our internal complexity such that we more smoothly interact with external complexity, which is what our VUCA world presents us with every day, essentially means that we evolve to a new level of consciousness. We "see with new eyes." To somewhat paraphrase my first poetry teacher, Jim Bodeen, "we die to live," through which metaphor he motivated receptive teenagers to transform themselves, dying to what they were that day so that they might be something greater the next. This is what we must do in order to evolve in alignment with the world around us.

What does it mean to evolve internal complexity? Alan Combs describes internal complexity as the number of perspectives available to a person. "Here we are talking about a kind of experiential landscape that maps the various ways persons can understand themselves and their surrounding world."[26] You might also think about this as changing the container of your mind, creating a bigger bucket to carry—often conflicting— ideas in.

As a result of having a range of ways of seeing things clearly, we immediately and instinctively select different data than we would have previously from the expanding amount of data around us. We make sense of things differently, and so we see, support, problem solve, and create differently.

This can result in many things, and I doubt I am going to be able to list them all here. It likely means that we will see opportunities for collaboration and cooperation where we previously saw only opportunities for competition. We will naturally take a dialogic stance in that we will be aware we have something to give and something to learn in all interactions and initially be confused when that is not welcome or wanted. But, we will retain our ability to engage in other forms of interaction while preferring and tending toward the dialogic. We will experience fear as information rather than a call to attack or defend. We will see conflict as a development opportunity. Our focus will be on the big picture and

Chapter 5: Consciousness Not Mindset

the value in the whole system. Our participation in the market will be one of ethical disruptive innovation. We will focus less on reporting structures and more on effective information flow to support high quality decisions as fast as possible. We will realize that our organizations are developmental spaces and be mindful of the kind of person we are sending back to the world at the end of the day.

We will welcome complexity in all things rather than trying to subdue it to simplicity. We will have learned the lesson that when we try to simplify that which is inherently complex, we build in more problems than we solve. We will welcome complexity as an opportunity to use our tools for engaging with complexity and for its benefit of helping us to develop our own internal complexity, learn, and mature so that we can welcome complexity with greater confidence and skill next time. And
we will recognize when complexity is not present and rely
on the appropriate tools and methods for the context we find ourselves in.

We will conceive of workplaces less as factories that make widgets and more as wellsprings of citizens wherein humans learn the craft of productive being. This is not necessarily a warm and fuzzy thing: I nearly gave you a metaphor of smelting. Knowledge-creating companies, such as software companies, might more appropriately function like research universities once did but with a more product- and service-oriented approach.

We will be drawn, as we mature, more toward transformation—not forgetting learning, but valuing development and the possibility of transformation more than learning. We will be alert to and understand where learning keeps us stuck more than helps us move to a higher level. This comment would seem to fly in the face of much of the standard rhetoric of agile coaches and consultants, so it's worth pausing here to clarify.

Discovery of "Mindset"

An interesting theory is has emerged over the last one hundred years about not only agile transformation but human transformation. This theory has been developed and elaborated by people such as Jean Gebser and Ken Wilber. In the last thirty years or so, theories of adult human development have been presented tested and found to have value. A major voice on this stage is Robert Keegan. Delving into both theoretical constructs shows resonances between them such that adult development appears to have a link with consciousness development.

In theories of adult development and consciousness evolution, each phase of development transcends and includes the phase before. There are resonances here with agile adoptions. And, since agile is primarily about people, it makes sense that the evolution of the humans would have a connection with the evolution of the adoption. For instance, in a given agile adoption, the organization may begin with a strict by-the-book Scrum process. Then, over a period of time, based on data gathered about flow and human thriving, the organization may evolve a model that includes all the value that Scrum brought them, but as they have mastered the complexities of their development process, that which looked complex now looks complicated or simple.

What's the Difference?

Put simply, a mindset you can take off and put back on again. A change in consciousness changes what you perceive and how you make sense of and relate to yourself, others, and the world around you. You can't take consciousness off at the end of the day; it's like having a new lens implanted on your cornea. Mindset is like a pair of glasses.

Chapter 5: Consciousness Not Mindset

According to the American Heritage Dictionary, to **learn** is:

1. a. To gain knowledge of or skill in through study, instruction, or experience: *learned how to sail; learned the new computer program; learn to speak Hindi.*

   b. To become aware or informed of; find out: *learned the truth about him; learned that it was best not to argue.*
   See Synonyms at discover.

2. To fix in the mind or memory; memorize: *learned the speech in a few hours.*

3. *Nonstandard* To cause to acquire knowledge; teach.

To **develop** is:

1. To bring from latency to or toward fulfillment: *an instructor who develops the capabilities of each student.*

2. a. To expand or enlarge: *developed a national corporation into a worldwide business.*
   b. To aid in the growth of; strengthen: *exercises that develop muscles.*
   c. To improve the quality of; refine: *develops his recipes to perfection; an extra year of study to develop virtuosic technique.*

3. a. To cause to become more complex or intricate; add detail and fullness to; elaborate: *began with a good premise but developed it without imagination.*
   b. *Music* To elaborate (a theme) with rhythmic and harmonic variations.

4. a. To bring into being gradually: develop a new cottage industry.
   b. To set forth or clarify by degrees: developed her thesis in a series of articles.

What's the Difference?

5. a. To come to have gradually; acquire: *develop a taste for opera; develop a friendship.*
   b. To become affected with; contract: *developed a rash; developed agoraphobia.*

6. To cause gradually to acquire a specific role, function, or form, as:
   a. To influence the behavior of toward a specific end: *an investigator who develops witnesses through flattery and intimidation.*
   b. To cause (a tract of land or a building) to serve a particular purpose: *developed the site as a community of condominiums.*
   c. To make available and effective to fulfill a particular end or need: *develop the state's water resources to serve a growing population.*
   d. To convert or transform: *developed the play into a movie.*

7. *Games* To move (a chess piece) to or toward a more strategic position.

8. a. To process (a photosensitive medium such as exposed film) in order to produce a photographic image.
   b. To produce (a photographic image) by use of a photosensitive medium or by printing from a digital file.

v.intr.
1. To grow by degrees into a more advanced or mature state: *With hard work, she developed into a great writer.*
   a. To increase or expand: *Sales developed until we needed a bigger warehouse.*
   b. To improve; advance: *Their skill developed until it rivaled their teacher's.*
2. To come gradually into existence or activity: *Tension developed between students and faculty.*
3. To come gradually to light; be disclosed: *reports the news as it develops.*

66

Chapter 5: Consciousness Not Mindset

A useful example from the definition of "develop" above is that of developing one's muscles. You don't add more information to your muscles, you change them in character as you develop them. Having developed your muscles, you are not only stronger, but you have likely picked up other characteristics such as better balance and, depending on how you have developed them, perhaps greater cardiovascular capability. You may also have increased your ability to focus and your overall stamina.

This is analogous to developing your internal complexity rather than simply learning. Learning can and often is related to increasing internal complexity, but learning can also keep us stuck at our current level of capability and internal complexity. This depends on the kinds of learning challenges presented to us. In particular, challenges with no known answers that contain an experiential component as well as personal risk tend to result in transformation that is based on increased internal complexity.

There are times in our lives when successful navigation of such challenges requires us to increase not only our learning but also our internal complexity. Relationships, whether personal or professional, can be transformative. Successful navigation of a divorce can be a positive and transformational experience resulting in us being truly different in the next relationship. Successful navigation of a work dislocation that results in us truly being different in the next work situation or in finding ourselves in an entirely different kind of work can also be evidence of increased internal complexity. Usually, people simply replay the same relationship script, seek the same employment, and, overall, attempt to employ the same strategies for success that resulted in the previous failed experience. Transforming takes more effort, can take more time, and can require that we traverse whatever your favorite change model*** is very consciously—in other

*** Many people like the Satir change curve. I tend to find a great deal of value in the Bridges model, possibly because he documented his own experience of his model so well late in his career as he experienced the death of his wife and his own transition to a new identity without her.

What's the Difference?

words, with a lot more awareness of the change. This requires courage, tenacity, and is most easily navigated within a supportive environment or with the support of at least one person who will stand by you when you confront the worst the developmental process has to offer you. Not all of us get this, and, as I will assert below, too much support can actually impede transformation.

In fact, the many mechanisms we put in place, from self-delusion to managerial processes that do not recognize and make use of the value of failure but, rather deny its existence, result in almost insurmountable impediments to true transformation. As a result, even those who were initially change agents powered by great energy and idealism, when faced with these impediments, are thwarted in both their desire to transform the organization and their need to transform themselves. They move into a sort of middle ground, jaded by their experiences, and often experience career or personal effects that lead to cynicism. And who can blame people for cynicism earned in such a manner—having come to do good, their intentions result in more harm than good, and they are older more than wiser, unless the wisdom of cautioning those who would try to not try is wisdom.

I wrote the following poem to exemplify the dialogue between those individuals and those they would caution about the futility of supporting positive change without insupportable personal cost.

Hunting the Heffalump

Down the gorgeous gorge of ignorance and innocence,
over the sandbar of apparent agreement
the flotilla of small craft sail without reluctance.
And we are them;
and we are in them.

Chapter 5: Consciousness Not Mindset

Under the stormy economic sky
floating the water of social change
the little armada charges bravely into the Wide World,
heedless of those who've gone before charting the same
course,
hunting for the Heffalump,
to kill it and bring it home.

Soon the watery deep knows them.
Soon the wind rises, the ocean rolls over
with a knowing smile.
Soon all hands are on deck with their souls in those hands.
Soon the old story is told:

The story of the bright, young dead;
the story of the scarred, bitter old.

Do not, do not build your ships in the sun
on the broad banks of the ancient river.
Do not, do not sail down the gorge,
give your life to the Heffalump hunt,
the survivors chorus.

But the bright young hear without listening.
They can navigate the sandbar of apparent agreement
bearing the flag of new understanding.
They fear neither sky nor water.

And the wise ocean knows
as the dark, deep being
rolls over and smiles.

    The point here is not that it is futile to follow your dreams for a better state of things. The point is that doing so is not without risk and many who have been there will try to dissuade you. They have their reasons. In this little book, I am suggesting you pack your backpack with an additional set of tools of a different type before you set out on the journey they're warning you away from.

Opportunities for Transformation and Self Transcendence

Much of what comes to us through the Agile Manifesto is social in nature. This may seem ironic to many people outside the software industry as they do not think of software developers as social people. Yet, much of what is in the agile frameworks and methods is actually social technology. To quote from an article I co-authored and which was published in 2016, "Socio-technology is the study of processes at the intersection of society and technology. Software development is as much about human interaction as it is about hardware configuration and coding languages. The technical practices are the tools and methods of a developer's social system. They are also examples of structured dialogues, both inter- and intrapersonal. Structured dialogue, as a sociotechnical practice, moves us along an evolutionary path toward greater consciousness."[27]

Individuals and interactions over processes and tools

Agilists can have broad-ranging, deeply reasoned, emotionally charged arguments about what constitutes valuing people over process and vice versa. In its fully realized form, valuing people over process can extend to deep democracy, collaboratively-led organizations that include such things as market placement, delivery targets, and high level organizational vision all being evolved through ongoing dialogue in organizations.

The kind of dialogue and power-sharing many agilists envision here means that line-level workers have only marginally less power—and perhaps no less power—over how the organization is run than does the C-suite. Hierarchies disappear in favor of networks, and decision making is done through both large and small group processes as opposed to any single individual having

Chapter 5: Consciousness Not Mindset

ultimate authority over others. The group is valued, some would say, even above individual needs. However, many agilists, including Jeff McKenna in *Conscious Software Development*, disagree. I align with those agilists. My understanding is that individuals are of great importance but not without reference to the community that is their context. McKenna says, "A lot of people who advocate agile methods sell the individual short, implying that we don't want individual contributors to stand out. That's not true at all—what is true is that we want people who are very conscious in their work."[28]

Working software over comprehensive documentation

While I have not witnessed or participated in many of these conversations, I could easily see people talking about the social value of documentation in comparison with the, to some, mind-numbing and soul-killing effects of creating that documentation. Some people might see it as disrespectful of others to not create documentation whereas others would see the creation of documentation as waste and therefore profligate use of time and human life energy.

Those who feel not creating documentation is disrespectful point to the loss of time in the future to relearn what was known in the past. However, those who advocate against documentation point to the fact that the greatest majority of documentation is never consulted again and that the time spent writing documentation could have been spent in more profitable ways, such as writing code or participating in retrospectives.

Customer collaboration over contract negotiation

Here is where the co-location, or face-to-face communication, tenet of agile first occurs. It is later emphasized in the principles, which you can flip back to and read in the preface. The importance of the human connection resounds in this value. Sometimes I've

Opportunities for Transformation and Self Transcendence

heard agilists interpret and summarize this as "conversations over contracts." Agilists can become very impassioned about the importance of live face-to-face conversations to establish expectations, clarify desires, negotiate differences, and establish, build, and maintain relationships. Agilists place a high value in people but, perhaps, an even higher value in relationships.

While the individual is priceless and the relationship could not take place without the individual, the relationship is greater than the sum of the individuals participating in it.

Responding to change over following a plan

This value, at first blush, appears to be focused very much on the needs of the profit-seeking business with its objective of adjusting to changing market conditions. But, actually, it is very much wrapped around the notions of estimation, commitment, and learning—especially learning. Project plans are created at the beginning of a project when we know the least about what we need to do in order to deliver the benefits intended by the project funders. When we don't adjust the plan as we learn about the nature of the work and how our tools are or are not a fit, we push the stakeholders closest to the project, the team delivering the business value, into a very tight spot. Sometimes, the feasibility of delivering the value slowly slips away when certain initial constraints are not flexed. This has predictably dire morale and engagement effects.

So, What Do We Make of This?

The "agile values" as those four bullet points in the Agile Manifesto are known, point to great potential for progressive human consciousness evolution, in fact, we can argue that they point to the importance of using agile values, principles, frameworks, and methods to evolve a new agile consciousness. Many people in the agile movement would argue that much needs to change, from the structure of work to the structure of organizations, from the

Chapter 5: Consciousness Not Mindset

way power is used to the way resources are distributed, even up to changing the purpose of business and organizations to be less money-focused and more human-focused. These things are not explicit in the manifesto and principles. But seventeen years of practice since the signing and publication of the Agile Manifesto, time spent in experimentation, analysis, and reflection, have convinced many people that these things are necessary.

Business theorists such as Gary Hamel, author of *The Future of Management*, and Steve Denning, author of *The Leader's Guide to Radical Management*, argue that not only does changing the way we lead and organize our work and organizations support agility but there is less waste than when we frequently force people and re-organize work groups. I have seen the wasteful fallout of reorganizations and layoffs—both from the organizational perspective and from the individual perspective—many times over the course of my career. From the productivity drain that is survivor syndrome among those left behind to the sometimes crippling self-esteem impacts of a summary dismissal during a mass layoff, in so many ways, the organization tells the individual—you don't matter. Management may even go so far as to say they are eliminating "waste" or "fat" during such a layoff.

Abandoning forcing and top-down re-organization as management tools requires a shift in how we think, our level of contextual awareness, what we notice, and what strategies and tactics we select as valuable and actionable. This kind of development as a leader tends to be based on increased knowledge of ourselves and others. It is the result of an enhancement in our understanding of how the world does work and can work and our place in that world, which is not to say our place in a pecking order but, rather, what the true scope of our influence is.

As Dee Hock says in *Birth of the Chaordic Age*, his memoir of the development of the VISA credit card system, a product and service development effort he led which revolutionized the banking system, "Understanding requires mastery of four ways of looking at things – as they *were*, as they *are*, as

So, What Do We Make of This?

they *might become*, and as they *ought to be*."[29]   The kind of understanding Hock talks about is the understanding of humans and our collective context. "Understanding" as Hock uses it here is related to the exploration and expansion of the current consciousness of a human system. Hock's questing mind (his autobiography is titled *Autobiography of a Restless Mind: Reflections on the Human Condition*) led him to create an organization ahead of its time using self-organizing methods ahead of their time. Using the perspective-evolving approach encapsulated by the four ways of looking at things cited above, he continually evolved his understanding of chaordic nature of organizations, which at any point in time embody aspects of both chaos and order.

The emergence of Carol Dweck's work on the growth mindset in 2007 was adapted for the agile community and introduced there by Linda Rising, co-author of *Fearless Change: Patterns for Introducing New Ideas*, at the Agile Alliance 2011 conference. The idea of an agile mindset has great power and has been successfully applied by many agilists to help teams shift away from a more mechanistic way of thinking about the organization of work, delivery of value, and relation to others. However, as has been the case with the application of servant leadership (see Appendix A), an agile *mindset* is not enough. The skill of being able to constantly learn is quite valuable. But, learning does not always help us develop our internal complexity which helps us move to a new way of seeing things, a new consciousness, awareness, and quality of noticing.

As Combs says in *Consciousness Explained Better*,

The basic idea here is that while experience has a vertical dimension set by a person's developmental stage, it also has a horizontal dimension represented by the number of perspectives available to that person. Here we are talking about a kind of

Chapter 5: Consciousness Not Mindset

experiential landscape that maps the various ways persons can understand themselves and their surrounding world.

Or, as Rob McNamara, author of *The Elegant Self, A Radical Approach to Personal Evolution for Greater Influence in Life*, says, it's important to be aware of the kind of learning opportunities that come your way. You can learn continuously without ever developing, or increasing internal complexity. Increasing internal complexity is what helps you cope with VUCA in your life, in the world, and in your organization.

And what is this internal complexity? Perhaps Combs describes it best given the brevity he employs:

*The theme of complexity continues to characterize mental growth, and with it the transformation of experience, as we encounter advanced stages of development. Here it is **not so much a matter of becoming smarter or more clever, but of acquiring flexible perspectives that are open to many facets of experience**[†††], and with them a growing attainment of creative and supple ways to relate to other people and address the day to day challenges we all face . . . The point here, however,*
is that growth at all levels of development is supported,
and to a significant degree created, by the blossoming of
internal complexity.

This kind of growth comes about from engaging with other people in ways that improve our awareness and noticing skills that increase our knowledge of ourselves and others. The kind of learning that helps us increase our internal complexity is the kind of learning that presents adaptive challenges rather than technical challenges. So, learning another coding language doesn't help much. However, learning another coding language with a partner with whom we must share power and resources and whose success we share in as they share in ours does help. It

---

††† Bolding is the author's.

So, What Do We Make of This?

presents us with many opportunities to learn about who we are and how we are in the world. It helps us increase our understanding of who they are and how they are in the world. It helps us evolve a better understanding of our collective and individual places in this world.

So, pursuing more learning of a technical sort doesn't help. Doing truly adaptive work does help us. A sign of doing that kind of work is that we're in conversation with others, because we can't generally solve adaptive challenges in the workplace on our own. A sign of having done a great deal of adaptive work is the range of lenses we're able to see the world through, to have, as one of my colleagues who'd been a citizen in four countries once said to me many "compatibility interfaces."

Chapter 6: What Helps Us Develop?

We often hear in agile circles that agile is all about learning. The cyclical communication processes and periodic retrospectives so that we can inspect and adapt our work processes focus us on learning. But, given that learning can keep us stuck and is different from development, how do we spot truly developmental opportunities and invest there rather than in more learning, which may not help us advance? Examples of learning that don't support development include learning more coding languages or more tools. Examples of a developmental opportunity include things like moving to a new team or taking on a technical or teambuilding challenge that we are not quite prepared for.

Overprotection as an Impediment

A colleague and I were talking a few weeks ago about the idea that Scrum Masters can over-protect teams and that this ultimately stunts the growth of the team. She has more than 15 Scrum Masters reporting to her and is in a position to see patterns across Scrum Master practice and its effect on teams—patterns very similar to what I have seen across organizations.

Now, before I go too far down this path, I want to acknowledge that being a Scrum Master is a very difficult job. Very little training is provided even to Scrum Masters who are certified, and much is expected of them. Their role is clearly defined in the *Scrum Guide*. How to fulfill that role is an ongoing quest for every Scrum Master I've ever met. And, that's as it should be.

Some years ago, at an Agile Open Northwest conference I wandered into a session on the risks of professionalizing the Scrum Master role. I've seen those risks manifest as issues. Some people take themselves very seriously in that role. It's a role without authority, but some Scrum Masters wield influence in a very heavy-handed way, while others are completely befuddled

Overprotection as an Impediment

about how to get the team's attention focused on the work and their rights and responsibilities, let alone accountabilities, as a Scrum team. Further, organizations sometimes hold the Scrum Master accountable for the success of the project or product delivery, which is a misapplication of accountability but which can make sense since this is such a new and different kind of role. It's a leadership role, but it's not a managerial role. This role facilitates the success of another role: the team.

Yet it must be acknowledged that how the Scrum Master functions with the team is a strong influencer on the team's successful evolution. For instance, some Scrum Masters protect the team from *everything*, including the natural consequences of their actions which result in failure. They seem to assume that all negative feedback is damaging. Actually, negative feedback and the experience of failure is a key driver of growth and development. To be protected from overwhelming or unfair negative feedback is useful. Not all negative feedback is harmful.

Every person makes meaning of the information they take in through their senses in a specific way that fits within a class of meaning-making known as a "quality of mind," or consciousness. As Robertson Davies said, "The eye sees only what the mind is prepared to comprehend."[30]

People create their world based on their form of mind, which includes their awareness and noticing skills. These skills tend to be linked with what they consider important information. Some people see themselves more as isolated individuals in the organization; some see themselves more as nodes in a network with a range of highly important relationships. The form of mind the organization has hired for and has optimized for, usually through a system of performance management, in turn informs the organization's ability to transform. Scrum Masters and agile coaches sometimes need to compensate for the organization's form of mind in relation to people.

Chapter 6: What Helps Us Develop?

When presented with change, the collective consciousness of the organization tends to respond with "that's not how we do things here" in many different ways and on many different levels. The organizational consciousness, which is similar to the culture but relies more on human connection than on cultural artifacts such as cubes and their placement, office art, or enterprise applications, is what pushes back against agile methods in many agile adoptions. This is why agile transformations are personal: They occur one individual at a time, even if those individuals sometimes transform in the context of a group, and many or all of the individuals in the group are transforming at the same time along the same path.

Feedback Supports Change

Negative feedback can drive adaptation of internal structures of consciousness and meaning with greater urgency than positive feedback. This is not an endorsement of creating opportunities for negative feedback or for focusing on that kind of feedback rather than positive feedback. It just acknowledges that there is value in experiencing the natural consequences of our words and actions, specifically there is value in the team's experiencing the consequences of their delivery or non-delivery to their stakeholders. The problem is that all too often our lack of focus on learning has resulted in more punishment than learning, which is counterproductive to improving autonomy or productivity. Our history of inappropriate distribution of accountability, specifically that we insist people be accountable for outcomes they cannot bound or ensure through their own words or action, has resulted in more authoritarianism in organizations than is good for the necessary evolution of the workforce as persons. And, protection of the team from the consequences of outcomes they have bounded and could extend control over is counterproductive to both their waking up and growing up.

Waking up and growing up are terms often used in the space of consciousness studies. Waking up is the moment at which you

Feedback Supports Change

realize that *who you are* in the world, *what the world is*, and *what your place in it is* are all very different than you thought. Growing up is the process of grappling with this new understanding, coming to terms with it, and integrating your new understandings into your updated operating system, or new level of consciousness.

To achieve actual development, as opposed to learning, we need to ensure we are confronted with that which is just beyond our current understanding or capability. For example, one shift in consciousness in the United States occurred when the residents of small town America began moving from the farms and small towns to the big cities to seek their fortunes in factories and larger businesses in the early twentieth century. They were confronted with people of very different cultures, a concept of time where the minutes mattered as much as the hours, a physical environment that blotted out the landscape, and work that could be repetitive and highly similar throughout the day rather than integrated into a system the way the farm or the small town they'd come from had been. To survive and be successful, they had to develop a whole new range of social and technical skills and often used these new skillsets simultaneously.

I had a moment over 25 years ago, sometime after I'd moved to a city from the small town I lived in. After not having been back to my home town in some months, I had the odd feeling that the top half of the town was missing as we drove down the main street because there were very few buildings over two stories tall. It left me feeling somewhat exposed and bereft, though in a few minutes I realized what the problem was. I had grown very accustomed to navigating a much denser, multi-story topography at a much more rapid pace. I needed to consciously switch back into the worldview of the people who lived in the small town, to their way of seeing time, valuing relationship over accomplishment, and their way of relating to food, gender, status, and social position. In that small town, my obvious female gender cast me in a very specific role, and it was not

Chapter 6: What Helps Us Develop?

"businessperson" or "software developer" as it was in the city. It was daughter, granddaughter, and niece; graduate of the east side high school; the one who moved away; and, essentially, the city person.

Developing is often a social challenge, not a technical one. After a certain point, it's also not technical from the perspective of being able to learn rules and protocols. There comes a point where rules and protocols almost subvert the intention to develop. It is in this way that the formal structures in the three predominant agile frameworks, Scrum, XP, and Kanban, actually begin to impede and stunt agility rather than evolve it. This is similar to the critique of the Project Management Institute Project Management Body of Knowledge, or PMI PMBOK, with its conservative and measured inclusion of thoroughly proven methods. Routine unquestioning practice of either type of model or method, whether predictive or adaptive, results in focusing on the model or method more than we focus on each other or the work. And, *that* is where the promise of development lies—in each other and the work.

The Agile Manifesto was all about each other and the work. *Each other*, in terms of the *people* the product was being created by and the people the product was being created for. *The work* in terms of *the product* and the *making of it*. And, the making of the product has great potency for the makers.

Double Loop Learning

Agilists are knowledge workers. Knowledge workers have certain common characteristics—and challenges. Research and theory development done by Christopher Argyris helps us understand why it is so difficult to do what we know we need to do in order to effectively pursue agility, to learn our way along the path to agility.

Christopher Argyris was a Yale educated Harvard professor and business theorist whose work focused on adult personality

Double Loop Learning

and action science, the study of how humans design their actions in difficult situations. Action learning is also a key academic research approach. Before his death in 2013 he contributed, with Donald Schon, the theory of double-loop learning that is so prized in the agile community. Additionally, he wrote excellent articles on learning and communication in the workplace such as "Teaching Smart People How To Learn" and "Good Communication That Blocks Learning."

Argyris coined the term "double loop learning" to distinguish it from single loop learning, which is mere correction of error when it is encountered. The advantage of double loop learning is that it can prevent errors in the future—before they occur.

As shown in Figure 1, double loop learning consists of two loops, the example above being one of the simplest illustrations

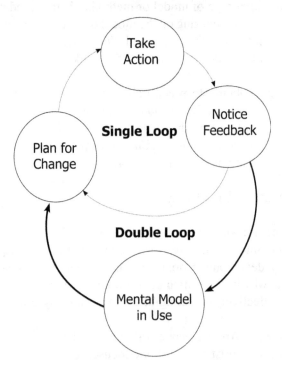

Figure 1 Illustration of Double Loop Learning

Chapter 6: What Helps Us Develop?

readily available. Single loop learning is shown in the top loop—take action, notice feedback, notice the gap between where you are and where you want to be (which constitutes the error), make a decision (which constitutes the fixing of the error), and start the loop again. Single loop learning tends to result in generating strategies and checklists to identify and fix the error more quickly the next time it occurs. Double loop learning adds the lower loop which is initiated at the "notice feedback" phase of single loop learning. At that point, the learner drops down into a reflective or reflexive mode that helps support the identification of mental models that may have motivated the actions that resulted in the error. This loop does not bypass the gap analysis but incorporates it into the reflexive evaluation of mental models. Mental models are the concepts we use to make sense of how things are in the real world.

Why This Kind of Learning is Hard for Us

While Argyris's work is invaluable, the following comment on "Teaching Smart People How to Learn" by Haridimous Tsoukas, a fellow academic and theorist, is one of the valuable passages I've read in relation to Argyris's work.

Titled "Vulnerability, Moral Responsibility, and Reflexive Thinking" the comment is rather lengthy, almost an article in its own right. When I first read it, I was struck by its applicability to the work agile-aspiring teams are involved in.

Tsoukas notes that the reason double-loop learning is so very difficult for knowledge workers is that this kind of worker is more vulnerable in reflexive, or double-loop, learning process than other kinds of workers. Their work is decision-intensive—thousands of micro-decisions per day, as we know—must be made by these workers. The results of these decisions evolve into the work product. When the work product and the processes that created it are scrutinized, the people who made the product are, therefore,

Why This Kind of Learning is Hard for Us

being scrutinized. And particularly when decisions made by a particular individual are scrutinized, it often feels to them as if they, personally, are being scrutinized, evaluated, and potentially found wanting.

Additionally, Tsoukas notes that people doing this kind of work exist in what he calls a post-modern firm. In the post-modern firm "individuals increasingly rely less on internalizing organizational authority as represented by the boss; instead, they rely more on internalized images of themselves, on their own personal authority."

Agile teams frequently function in bureaucratic hierarchies that they are trying to navigate or free themselves from to remove impediments to their functioning. In the course of doing so, they are often coached to understand how much of the power they have placed outside themselves, in their supervisor and the organization, is actually within them. And, they may be coached about the importance of assuming that power again.

Tsoukas uses the term "psychologically present" to describe the state of the knowledge worker in the informated[‡‡‡], post-modern firm, where hierarchical authority is increasingly less helpful in getting work done. He highlights the fact that double-loop, or reflexive, learning that Argyris advocates is prized in this kind of firm, and it also means that "the more informated a workplace is, the more reflexive the organization is capable of becoming . . . it has the opportunity to feed back, and reflect on, the information about its modus operandi and the outcomes it brings about." This means that, if the workers become skillful at reflexive thinking, or

---

[‡‡‡] "Informated" is a term coined by Shoshanna Zuboff in her book *The Age of the Smart Machine* (1988) to describe the process that translates descriptions and measurements of activities, events and objects into information. This process makes these activities visible to the organization and can be used to monitor what Zuboff calls human agency, or the individual's ability to act on their own behalf and for their own purposes.

Chapter 6: What Helps Us Develop?

double-loop learning, the organization has a tremendous asset in that it can adjust to what is learned very quickly.

Below Tsoukas coincidentally describes the challenge of engaging in effective retrospectives in agile teams.

In such organizations, individuals need to be able to ask critical questions of others and of themselves if they are to be effective in fully reaping the potential benefits reflexivity brings about. Individuals, therefore, no longer need to uphold the "masculine ideal"—that is, to suppress doubt and ambivalence. On the contrary, doubt, debate, and reflexivity are the very qualities needed to promote learning. A knowledge-intensive workplace thrives on the exchange of ideas and experiences in the interest of enhancing the collective pool of knowledge and of generating new ideas.

Tsoukas discusses the shift in affect that is required on an effective agile team. They are not a group of experts working together, each contending for his or her expert perspective. They are a team of generalizing specialists that is collaborating around a common vision and goal.

*. . . Throughout his work, Argyris has pointed out the difficulties practitioners have in engaging in reflexive thinking—in his terms, in "double-loop thinking." This is particularly so in the case of knowledge workers because, **to the extent they are more psychologically present at work, they expose more of themselves to others; hence, they are more vulnerable.** Argyris documents this vulnerability in his article, showing the defensive reasoning it brings out in knowledge workers. More than that, however, he shows what individuals need to do in order to stop being defensive when the spotlight is turned on themselves—how to engage in productive reasoning. The message Argyris is getting across, it seems to me, is not only how productive reasoning may be*

Why This Kind of Learning is Hard for Us

*achieved but, also, **the importance of constantly challenging yourself, of expanding your horizons, of "knowing thyself."***

*In other words, Argyris invites knowledge workers to undertake a primarily moral, not just technical, task: to be open to criticism, to be willing to test their claims publicly against evidence, **to accept that they too are partly responsible for the problems they are confronted with**[§§§] . . . It all comes down to individual responsibility, and this is, essentially, a moral issue. In that sense, as well as being an influential organizational psychologist and an implicit moral philosopher, Argyris is a systemic theorist, not too different from his own hero Gregory Bateson (1979): we partly create the problems we face, he says, and we have a responsibility for this. An excellent point.*

In order to develop, we must engage in double-loop learning. This kind of learning in software development often comes close to who we think we are in the world, how we think the world is, and what our place in the world. All these understandings of ours tend to get challenged in this learning process. Skillful conversations can support "aha" moments in us that move us away from the corrosion of character and toward greater internal complexity.

Self-Development as Service

Much is made of the servant leadership model among agilists. Yet many agilists who tout this model have never read Robert K. Greenleaf's essay, "The Servant as Leader,"[31] which describes it. So, the model is often, I might even go so far as to say, usually, misunderstood and misapplied. It is clear from a reading of that essay that servant leaders cannot self-identify, though many do in the agile community. You know that a servant leader is present because the context they are in, or "those led" as Greenleaf, the

---

[§§§] Bolding is the author's.

Chapter 6: What Helps Us Develop?

creator of the Servant Leadership model, puts it, pass what is known in the servant leadership community as "the best test." The best test is:

Do those served grow as persons? Do they, while being served, become healthier, wiser, freer, more autonomous, more likely themselves to become servants (first)?

To manage and develop oneself is, in this world, an act of servant leadership. Since all agile transformation is personal transformation, she who is in most need of transformation *first* and in an ongoing fashion is the change agent (agile coach, Scrum Master, or agile advocate) themselves. The amount of learning that is required in an agile transformation is prodigious. If, therefore, learning is not associated with joy, even if it is sometimes painful or arduous, then learning will not likely happen except through crisis, such as a reorganization resulting in massive work dislocation. It may not even happen then if the response to the crisis is one of victimhood. The greatest service that we who aspire to and adore agility can provide to others is to learn out loud. In other words, we must truly engage in ongoing transformation before the eyes of those in whom we would inspire transformation. This means that we risk expulsion from our community as we traverse the developmental path. We can come to look less like them. They may want us to "change back," merely pick up a new kind of air guitar, and strum along with them.

The work of personal development, socially speaking, is therefore easier said than done. Especially if we define our sense of diversity narrowly.

Some adult development coaches, such as Rob McNamara, author of *The Elegant Self*, believe that transforming to the next level of consciousness—from wherever you are—takes

Self-Development as Service

on average ten years. It makes sense to me that a moment of waking up followed by years of integration of that experience, or growing up, can be shorter than ten years depending on the power of the original waking up experience and the diligence of the integrative work.

Triple Loop Learning

Beyond double loop learning lies triple loop learning and, some argue, the path to wisdom and even potentially self-transcendence. Along the way is a type of learning that can test our sense of belongingness and try others' notions of our integrity. It's a steep road, but it is well worth climbing in the long run. And, it is, after all, the road we are asking organizations and teams to climb.

Early on in my education, my mother introduced me to the notion of personal enrichment. Personal enrichment was education and experiences you secured for yourself simply in order to be a more interesting person and have a more interesting life without any vocational motivation whatsoever. For instance, you might travel, learn Brazilian embroidery, take a sketching class or a class on ancient textiles as I did as I was growing up. Learning entirely new things just for the "broadening" experience of it was seen as good for me. And, it turns out that it was. I know all kinds of crazy stuff that comes in handy when I find myself growing bored in or out of company.

Had these learning experiences challenged my values, sense of who I was, beliefs about my very beingness then they would have possibly engaged me in triple-loop learning. In very small ways, a couple of them did: my very brief exposure to Brazilian embroidery challenged my thinking about embroidery as a two-dimensional craft as opposed to a three-dimensional art form. The sketching class taught me that I, perhaps, did not need to be imprisoned only in words for self-expression: I had some small ability to sketch.

Chapter 6: What Helps Us Develop?

Triple-loop learning takes a giant leap beyond this kind of perspectival shift. It looks beyond the mental models evaluated by double-loop learning and reflects on the values, attitudes, beliefs and presence of the actor. It asks us to make an existential re-evaluation. It asks us to consider our existential goals and whether our beingness aligns us with success for those goals. It supports us in developing wisdom.

Below is a diagram that shows the relationship of single, double, and triple loop learning. This diagram makes clear the interdependence of the three approaches to learning. The third loop is truly developmental in nature. This is, to my mind, where the best agile coaches spend the greatest amount of their time.

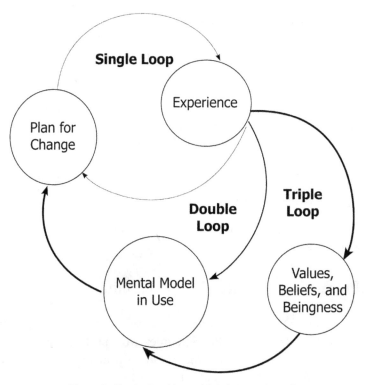

Figure 2: Single, Double, and Triple Loop Learning

Triple Loop Learning

The incremental learning process we tout so often is single loop learning. The reflexive learning, which takes place most often in retrospective meetings or moments, lives in the double-loop learning. However, triple-loop learning is where we truly evolve our beingness toward a social reality where true agility lives. Double-loop learning asks that we pause and reflect. Triple-loop learning asks that we change in the moment, even at the values level, and welcome unpredictable and uncontrolled learning.

Markus Peschl shows the link between triple-loop learning, individual cultivation, and wisdom. He asserts that "if one is interested in profound change a *new level*, implying a new dynamics, has to be introduced; profound change does not only happen in the cognitive domains."[32] This kind of profound change is what we are asking of organizations and teams as we coach and encourage them to pursue true agility. We coach most effectively when we coach from experience as well as theory. Peschl goes on to make another interesting point:

> *Whereas it is possible to "play games" on the cognitive/ intellectual level (in the sense of trying out or simulating intellectual positions without being touched essentially by them), on can experience that there exists a level, where "intellectual games" are not possible any more. We are then confronted with a level going beyond the domain of cognitive or intellectual questions touching the self at the very center.*[33]

Air guitarists can't play this tune. The guitar must be present in order to be played.

Presencing As Triple Loop Learning

Much of the remainder of Peschl's paper summarizes Scharmer's Theory U. Otto Scharmer, MIT professor and author of *Theory U: Leading from the Future as it Emerges*, has created a detailed grammar of social technology of personal and large

Chapter 6: What Helps Us Develop?

systems transformation called presencing that has great value. Coaches who are pursuing personal and systems transformation can benefit greatly from reading this book. Peschl essentially argues that Theory U, and therefore Scharmer's grammar of social change, is a well-mapped approach to triple-loop learning. This is of interest to agilists, who typically work with knowledge workers and especially software developers because the context in which they are enacting change is *socio*technical.

Scharmer in *Theory U: Leading from the Future as It Emerges* focuses on the leader as change agent facilitating change in organizations by focusing on moments that are ripe for change. Scharmer adopts the view of "the human being as a being of freedom—as a being that is defined by the capacity to make the choice between acting in habitual ways and connecting with one's deepest source of creativity, ethical action, and freedom".[34] This is reminiscent of Greenleaf's hallmark of the servant leader as causing followers to become progressively "healthier, wiser, freer, more autonomous" (Greenleaf, 1991, p. 13). Scharmer describes Theory U as the social technology of presencing and asserts that each individual and community is two selves, that which we have become as a result of our journey from past to present and the dormant self, the one waiting to be born as a result of presencing. "Presencing is the process of connecting these two selves. To connect our current with our authentic self. To move toward our real self from the future" (p. 189). Presencing is grounded on the systems thinking principle of emergence, a systems thinking principle which relates to the way complex systems arise out of relatively simple interactions (see Corning, 2002). On page 236 Scharmer specifically links emergence with presencing as "deep social emergence".

In *Theory U*, Scharmer develops his theory of leadership through the process of presencing into five movements: co-initiating, co-sensing, co-presencing, co-creating, and co-evolving.

Presencing As Triple Loop Learning

Within each of these movements is a set of principles and practices to actualize the movement, twenty-four principles and practices in all (see Appendix A). The principles and practices, which are detailed in the text, provide the leader with both guidance and a container for their practice, which Scharmer characterizes as a specific kind of deep listening which allows the leader to identify the future that wants to emerge for a specific organization and then lead from that perspective.

Scharmer details three voices which impair the movement up the "U:" the Voice of Cynicism, the Voice of Fear, and the Voice of Judgment. The Voice of Judgment is seen as an inner enemy of the Self which blocks the gate to the open mind. The Voice of Cynicism is the enemy that blocks the gate to the progress of the Self on the journey to the authentic Self, that is, confronting the questions "What is my self?" and "What is my work?" The Voice of Fear is the third enemy that blocks the gate to the open will, which prevents the Self from letting go of what we have and who we are in order to allow emergence to occur.

Four fields of conversation, and in this case "field" refers indirectly to field theory, used to navigate from one movement to another in the journey down and back up the "U" are "downloading" or "talking nice" which is also known as politically correct speech; "debate" or "talking tough"; "dialogue" or "reflective inquiry"; and "presencing" or "generative flow." The four fields of conversation are among the twenty-one propositions of social field theory Scharmer covers in his chapter on the detailed grammar of the social field, a crash course on how social interaction constructs human reality when that reality is instantiated in a group. Through this chapter, Scharmer provides a number of different detailed slices of Theory U which are essentially sets of tools to help the reader enter a human system and navigate the social field in a manner that will allow the system to move through the five movements of the U. In Appendix B, I provide a brief summary of Scharmer's 531-page masterwork.

Chapter 6: What Helps Us Develop?

CDAI As Triple Loop Learning

I began to formally study human conflict in the late 90s. Early on, I became interested in collaboration, though most of my life had been dominated by competition. The model I worked with primarily was the Thomas-Kilmann model. I intuited that the collaborative mode had the greatest potential in evolving consciousness. This is validated by Nicolaides and McCallum's research on CDAI, Collaborative Developmental Action Inquiry.[35]

CDAI, though created by Torbert, is related to the practice of adaptive leadership, a learning-based leadership model created by Heifetz and his associates, which is ideally suited to leaders in agility aspiring environments. It requires that the leader be willing to act as a learning facilitator who is not afraid to both keep the followers safe enough to learn and stressed enough to bring out their best thinking. A key tool in this model is "get up on the balcony," wherein the leader switches perspective rapidly from the metaphorical dance floor where the followers and the work is, to the balcony, where she can get a whole systems view of the work and the leadership challenge. This is a very demanding—and growth-inspiring—form of leadership. It requires of the leader that they recognize that their role is to help facilitate both growth and meaning-making in the context of the problem which has introduced confusion and challenge in the first place:

To attain and sustain these levels of meaning making and learning in action, a leader recognizes and remains in relationship with (1) intuition, intention, and attention; (2) critical and strategic thinking; (3) vigilant and meaningful actions; and (4) impacts, outcomes, and feedback.[36]

There is great value in the human experience of encountering each other so as to smooth our rough edges. The challenges here are two-fold: (1) can we transform ourselves based on what we learn of the world and our fellow travelers so as to stay in integrity and retain our sense of personal agency, and (2) can we recognize and welcome the fact of difference while transforming rather than demanding conformance to a homogenizing norm?

I commented earlier in this book about the value of negative feedback. I want to acknowledge that, yes, it can be delivered in a crushing way. However, I have received value from negative feedback, even from the agile community. Because, frankly, I must acknowledge that agilists, even prominently placed agilists, have not always been supportive or even kind to me. Rather, they have manifested in all their humanity, sometimes identifying me as a competitor, sometimes as a troublemaker who's perhaps no better than she should be; and sometimes as a true fellow traveler and advocate.

In the not too distant past, I've had tremendous learning experiences that have highlighted and tested my values in the context of collaboration. I've studied collaboration in the context of the Thomas-Kilmann model for nearly twenty years now, and it was in that context that I had the first inklings of what collaborative work could do for us as individuals and even as a society. I also see value in other models, though the Thomas-Kilmann model seems the most complete, specific, and portable in my experience.

When speaking publicly or to teams where I am new, I've often asked about the experience of being collaborated on. True collaboration requires that we focus on shared interests, be in dialogue about those interests, and engage in the work together, whether or not we are truly working simultaneously. There is a theory of collaboration that says that everyone must be involved in creating the original set of interests that brought the collaboration into being in order for collaboration to be present. It has always seemed to me that skilled agilists would have strong collaborative

Chapter 6: What Helps Us Develop?

capability so that, when they joined an effort in flight or engaged with a client to coach, they would be able to spot pre-existing interests with which they could align at least as much as they might ask for new interests to be considered. This may seem counter-intuitive given that this whole discussion has been about transformational change. So, for example, know that I am talking about situations in which deep common interests are at issue.

An agile software developer who also sees herself as an agile advocate joining a team in a cybersecurity company may align with the interest of keeping private information private—and using agile methods to do so. An agile coach engaging with a client who is only doing predictive projects may align with the interest of ensuring the viability of the organization and preserving the income of its employees—and using agile values, principles, and practices to do so. An executive joining a company to turn around the low productivity and poor market alignment of the organization may align with the interest of ensuring the organization continues to exist, becomes a go-to employer, and is profitable—and using agile values, principles, and practices to do so. Checking out interest alignment is key when we engage on a new effort and re-validating that alignment is key for a healthy collaboration—even under difficult circumstances.

In one case, I was asked to ensure that a state government initiative to monitor the prescription of certain drugs was enacted. My role was to coach a new sponsor in the sponsorship role and to ensure that a third-party vendor was selected to implement the software. I was working with internal stakeholders who were not aligned politically with this very hot project. I recognized their internal stress regarding the implementation of this software and focused on the fact that legislation had been passed by elected representatives to support this software implementation. The common interests we aligned around were professionalism in carrying out the will of the legislature; due diligence in the selection process; transparency in the project; and timeliness in supporting the initiative as written. My assumption, which I re-validated continuously with these stressed stakeholders, was that participation in the project was voluntary. Many times, we had to re-validate our common interests as we proceeded through this challenging task. I learned that collaboration can be a pretty rough experience at times. I learned that I have skills I don't always care to use.

In another case, I was working with a colleague to generate a new article related to agile. We had a shared interest in creating this work around a thesis we felt would have great benefit to the agile community. While working together in real time, we generally collaborated swimmingly—shockingly well. However, a difference around keeping short term commitments to each other evolved in concerns on my part about whether respect was present in the relationship. Then we discovered late in the cycle that we had a philosophical difference about a key aspect of the thesis. I learned that I have strong standards about professionalism that are not only deep rooted but also can cause me to evaluate character unfavorably when those standards are offended. I learned that there should *always* be an emergency exit clause in any collaboration, and that this should probably be documented and revisited frequently. I learned that retrospectives early and often, even in dyadic relationships are important. And I learned that professional relationship was different than I thought it was, and I learned a bit about boundaries.

I have come to believe that it is difficult to be a good agile coach if you are not participating in some similar sort of growth experience. There are precious client experiences where this can happen, but they are rare. There are personal relationships where this can happen, but they are not as common as would be good for us. I do believe that treasured colleagues can partner in our

Chapter 6: What Helps Us Develop?

growth in this way, but I do not see this kind of growth in far too many agile coaching communities, to the extent that I have been able to participate or have observed them. All too often, we succumb to the talking head, the adulated air guitarist, or the mutual admiration society with everyone reading the same thing and nodding at the same time.

It is up to you to decide what you will do with your one wild and precious life. You walk the earth as an example to others no matter what you do. That's worth thinking about.

Chapter 7: Your Own Agile Heart

As I write this, there is another Agile Alliance global conference in flight this year in Orlando. Many people have gathered to share ideas, seek information, and propose solutions to the problems they see in their workplace and their world. Many of the attendees will be going for the first time this year. Some have been attending for many years. I know I am not alone in my sense of "stuckness" regarding the agile movement. Some of this year's attendees and I have had conversations specifically about this.

Perhaps we have forgotten that we can change any system we have created. We certainly created the agile movement. We can help each other out of the mire we have guided ourselves into. We must each begin, first, with ourselves.

Self-Care in a Troubled World

This is self-care in a troubled world. Self-care means time alone in contemplation to reflect and integrate what we're learning in our practice and to let our heads empty. A cacophonous mind cannot be present to the client and struggles to pay attention and to learn from experience. Self-care also means time for reading and study so that we may make progress in our understanding of all that underlies our work. Because learning in community helps keep us honest about our progress, self-care also means time together working and supporting each other through developmental challenges. "Worldwork," as Arnold Mindell, author, teacher, facilitator, physicist, and Jungian analyst calls it, is urgent, demanding, challenging and transformative. We do not lead agile transformations, which I believe falls in the category of worldwork, without first having proceeded down the path of transformation ourselves. Agilists are called upon to do worldwork if they want to see the kind of wholesale change in business and organizations that will allow us to successfully live in a VUCA world.

Agile coaches, consultants, and advocates are particularly accountable, by implication, to draw from reserves of personal development in times of stress. Research shows that, in times of anxiety and confusion, even adults regress to earlier levels of development. Not only do people come into the workplace with certain stressors and preoccupations already layered on from the world around them, but there will necessarily be times when the work environment seems to come apart, as well. At times like this, it is particularly important for the coaches and champions leading the way to agility to continue to model good agile cultural standards and practices. Even one person's example has a calming and centering effect on others and helps the observer both remember their commitment to agility and realize that maintaining that commitment is possible even under difficult circumstances.

For agile coaches and champions, the motivation toward self-development and self-care may be found in their desire to see the cultural outcomes that agile prefigures. It is important that we both model these outcomes and ensure we have the vim and vigor to work for them. For far too many people, the reality of work, which makes up most of their waking hours is much as it is for the speaker in the poem below. I have seen agile coaches and consultants driven so hard on the road that they do not at all provide their best to their stakeholders. Sometimes, they hardly seem to know which way is up!

Work

To be glad for work
that there is work
to fill the days

Chapter 7: Your Own Agile Heart

and nights,
work to fill the time
we must be alive
and work to fill the work.
Whatever the work is
it is work that we can do,
work that we may be, may breathe
work that we may forget ourselves
receive permission to be,
indulgence.

Or fear and dread the work
that we must work at and
knowing it is work—
but, work is work and
we must go to work.
Work we dread that is unpleasant
but work we must to drag home
the roof, the haunch, the heat
in the cold. Work that is work,
just work and nothing but
work.

But what is a man—
or woman—without work
the routine, the daily task list
from the Taskmaster who receives
a bigger list from her Taskmaster,
a list of work that must be worked,
that must be worked and worked
until there is no work.
Then we sit in dread until

Work

there is work, more work,
and we work and work
to receive indulgence, permission,
the haunch, the heat,
our reward for working at this
work.

The sentiment of this poem is the reality for far too many people in our society. Don't let it be yours. For those in this state, the impact extends to the whole experience of their lives, their community of influence, and the broader society.

A Lesson Firmly Taught

The formative value and privilege of working was impressed upon me at a young age.

When I was in the third grade, I had a fantastic teacher. Her name was Miss Eileen Ryan. She was a no-nonsense woman who climbed mountains, related to children as responsible human beings, and taught me to love learning again. She was both structured and supportive in her approach, and she didn't tolerate riotous behavior in her classroom. She was a marked change from Mrs. Goldsmith in whose classroom I was quite miserable. (I remember she told my mother I might never learn to read.) Miss Ryan wore bright red lipstick and had a broad smile that lit up her eyes with sparkles.

One day, in response to a recalcitrant class who didn't want to do their lessons she said, "Okay, who here doesn't want to have to work tomorrow?" Having been taught to speak up for what I thought from a young age, I raised my hand—as did my best friend, Bonnie, and one hapless little boy. I think his name was Mark. Miss Ryan said, "Fine. You don't have to work at all

Chapter 7: Your Own Agile Heart

tomorrow." We had just learned the scientific definition of "work" at the time: "To apply force against an object."

The next day, we all came to class and sat at our desks as normal when the bell rang. Miss Ryan declared that we three would be excused from work all day. In fact, we would be allowed to sit quietly at our desks, while others worked. No need to do 15-minute timed multiplication drills. No need to read aloud in social studies. And, worst of all, no chance to go to the back of the room where the workbench with lightbulbs, switches, and wires could be formed into circuits to one's heart's content while the breeze blew gently through the open multipaned windows that looked out through the leafy, swaying tree branches. We three went to lunch and sat with the other children at the lunch table then came back to the classroom and waited for class to begin. At the end of the day, we collected our belongings from the cloak room, went home, and returned changed beings.

I suspect Miss Ryan was a very vital woman outside of her workplace. I know she climbed Mount Rainier, and I believe she climbed Mount Si several times. She moved with joy and purpose, and I only remember her frowning when things weren't going well in the classroom. She would say "People! People!" and clap her hands sharply if things were really getting out of hand.

My father did work he hated for most of his life. He was an electrician who wanted to be a farmer. Farmers are called upon to do much creative problem solving. At the time, my family lived on a working farm. This was before factory farming and just before the advent of corporate farming. A farmer and his family could create something of great value out of the ground using their wits, skills, and hard work. They could do all this together while having the freedom of working outdoors every day, which for some people, I realize is not attractive. The need to provide medical

A Lesson Firmly Taught

benefits for us children meant that my father worked as a union electrician except for a brief two-year period in my adolescence which ended abruptly when the barns were torched.

Seeing him miserable in his work week after week, year after year, trapped in jobs where he crawled through spaces that were too short or too small for him, working in the mud for someone else's ultimate benefit, coming home unhappy in his work, and experiencing the effects of his unhappiness on our family definitely had its effect on me. Yet the creative and contributive value of working and providing value to one's community and independence for oneself was also clearly communicated. In fact, part of being a grownup was working. It conferred the status of adulthood. It meant you were now a contributing member of society, not a burden on anyone.

It has always been my understanding that the ability to work was a joy as much as an obligation. And, somehow, probably through multiple experiences, it became clear to me that work could be a calling and also that it inevitably formed who we were. Because of my love of learning, I wanted to do work that meant I would always be learning. I was fortunate enough to find work that required this, and while it has been a joy, it has occasionally been a challenge.

Working in the software industry meant that I was part of a profession that encountered the values and principles of agile sooner than many others. For much of my career, I've thought of going to work as going to school. As a coach and consultant, I find myself learning at least as much as I teach any client. These experiences with them form and inform me. The challenges they have that we work through together press me forward to learn more about myself, others, and the world we have created through the system of agreements we've made.

Chapter 7: Your Own Agile Heart

A Moment of Personal Change

Since work forms and informs us, and since knowledge workers are so very integrated with their work because they make the product very much out of themselves—their own brain cells, so to speak, it follows that work can be a context for consciousness evolution or the stunting of that evolution. Waking up can happen quickly, as in a near-death experience—or it can slowly dawn on you. I've had a number of waking up experiences through my work. Some have been quite memorable. And, so have you, I'm sure.¶¶¶

One such moment for me occurred in 2002 during the tech sector restructuring. I had been the sponsor for a small, free conference held at a local university to help technical communicators understand that their jobs were likely to be combed out of the tech economy and how to repurpose their skills to other kinds of work. After I led that day-long conference, I began to regularly get calls from unemployed technical writers who needed someone to listen to them.

One day, I received three calls from three men, all of whom had children. In two cases, I could hear the children playing in the background. In one case, he was about to go pick up his children from school and daycare. In all three cases, these men were, I realized, telling me fears that they could not share with their wives. They had all been looking for work for many months, and they felt they were out of options. It was not simply a matter of lack of income, it was a matter of a confused and unhappily changing identity, from valuable contributor to one more unemployed guy in a faceless sea of many. Years later, Scott Simon, commentator on National Public Radio's Weekend Edition Sunday, wrote a brief essay on the Labor Day experience of the involuntarily

---

¶¶¶ If you haven't thought through this before, it's worthwhile to take a few minutes to do so now. There are guiding questions in Appendix A to help you.

A Moment of Personal Change

unemployed American called "They'd Trade Labor Day for Days of Labor," that described perfectly what I was seeing at that time.[37]

Up to that point, I had been a very competitive consultant in my field. I could easily size up the competition, spot their weak point, educate myself into it, and seize the opportunity. Generally, from the point at which I decided I wanted to pick up a project inside a company and the day I signed the contract, I could count 90 days. That wasn't bad from a standing start. However, at this point in my career, I was also functioning more as a "small c" consultant rather than a "big C" consultant. In other words, I worked on specific sets of deliverables more often than I provided strategic services.

I remember sitting at my desk after that last phone call looking out the window and thinking about what I had heard, the differences and the remarkable similarities among those men. And, I experienced a sudden and intense shift of value from aggressive competitiveness to get the most for myself toward a desire for a more collaborative approach so that everyone might get all their most important needs met. It happened within a few minutes. It was not a near-death experience or a high of any sort. It was more like a strong, dawning realization that split me down the middle head to foot and moved outward through my understanding and values structure. It gave me a different perspective on how I had been and how I wanted to be. It felt like a call to action on a very broad scale. And, at a certain level, I haven't been the same since. This does not mean that I've never exhibited competitive behavior since. But it does mean that I've been more aware of doing so and have had a stronger preference for and fascination with collaboration.

In the few years prior to that moment, I had learned about and begun to practice the Thomas-Kilmann Conflict Modes model.[38] Just learning that there were at least five ways of engaging in a conflict was of value to me. And for years before that day on the

Chapter 7: Your Own Agile Heart

telephone, I had been seeing the metaphorically bloody aftermath of downsizings and restructurings as I often picked up projects left orphaned by related staff changes. These learnings and experiences combined with that moment had a profound effect on me. They motivated me to be different and therefore notice things I wouldn't otherwise have noticed. That moment helped increase my self-awareness. Those conversations that day helped me increase my knowledge of Self and Other.

From what I have seen, growing up is a matter of study through any of a variety of sources including dialogue, self-reflection, contemplation, and, in general, rubbing up against the reality of being of both human and non-human animals. I would even go so far as to say that the organism that is the earth qualifies as a teacher, but in the city, where most of us live these days, it can be harder to perceive the planet's being—and easier to take it for granted.

Agile values, principles, and practices, if practiced appropriately provide many opportunities not only for learning but for waking up. They also require more self-mastery, peer support, and supportive organizational context than exists for many agile teams. Making it your purpose and work to pursue the conditions for this kind of agile practice is a great act of service as well as likely a great opportunity for true growth and development on your part.

Even in a context in which agile adoptions have failed to sustain themselves multiple times, you can practice the values and principles at your own desk, which may be all the sphere of influence you have.

Your Life as Your Playground

To successfully lead a transformation, I have become convinced, we must first transform ourselves. And, we must

Your Life as Your Playground

put in place practices for ourselves to sustain and further our transformation. There are many pointers to this fact, but the outcome of the transformation can be counter-intuitive. For one thing, the outcome may not look the same for everyone.

Your own wild and precious life is your playground. Certainly, you have duties and obligations. The world needs more grownups. Be one—with a sense of humor. But, still, in any given day, you can run experiments and see what kind of results you get. You can drive to work along a different route. Were you more alert when you arrived? You can kiss your beloved on the other cheek. Was the effect more noticeable? You can ask someone else to lead the retrospective for the team you serve, your client, or your project so you can sit in and participate—or step out and get candid feedback later. Did you learn more as a result? You can advocate for the adoption of key technical practices such as pairing and collective code ownership, or you can just casually ask team mates to pair with you. Is your work more enjoyable? Do you solve problems faster? Observe, reflect, and see what's there for you.

You can read a difficult book at the edge of your expertise. You can switch roles with someone you are working with. You can become active in your local community advocating for peace, patients' rights, high quality drinking water, the restoration of the liberal arts in high school curriculum, or provide free critical thinking skills classes for adults. If you usually lead, follow.

If you haven't spent a day with toddlers in some years, give a young parent a break—and think about your experience with that child and what you learned when you're tucked up with your cup of tea that night. To what extent are you still that toddler?

We speak to each other of the value of "beginner's mind" in our work. But, usually, we succumb as coaches and consultants to the expert trap. Don't our clients, whether internal or external, depend on us for that expertise? Or, is it that they depend on us

Chapter 7: Your Own Agile Heart

for the demonstration of some expertise but, even more vitally, the presence of an agile consciousness? I think this is, indeed, more the case. I am to the point in my career where I am approached for mentoring by others more junior. This can surprise me when it happens. When I look back on my career, it looks more like a long road of stumbling, falling, getting up again, tending my wounds (sometimes too long), and starting off again. I often tell people I have just followed my nose, doing what I have to do to stay in integrity, learn as much as I can about my world, and help where I can.

The following poem describes my experience as best I could at the time I wrote it. I hope it inspires you to keep following your nose, as well.

I Rushed Forward

> Tell me, what else should I have done?
> Doesn't everything die at last, and too soon?
> Tell me, what is it you plan to do
> with your one wild and precious life?
> Mary Oliver
> "The Summer Day"

This was all the encouragement I required:
a sidelong glance, a paycheck:
I rushed forward.

Adventure was enough,
the mere promise of new and more experience—
this was all the encouragement I required.

No prescience of harm to mind, body, or spirit
could slow my lusting curiosity.
I rushed forward.

Your Life as Your Playground

Though others failed, I might succeed
and, if nothing else, have been there.
This was all the encouragement I required.

Should—can I regret now
looking back that
I rushed forward?

The new sun shines pink and gold
through the roses on my bedroom curtains.
This was all the encouragement I required.
I rushed forward.

For agilists who have witnessed multiple unsustained adoptions, "what is it you plan to do with your one wild and precious life?" can be a very potent question. People, focused on greater freedom and autonomy, interested in a good economic life for themselves and their community, aware of the joy and, now, the imperative of learning and development, people focused on moving everyone forward—these people have existed well before the Agile Manifesto was ever conceived of. You may see yourself as one of them. Many things came together to provide the resources we have to draw on as agilists today. It is coincidental that software development existed as a profession and many people who are interested in the developmental power of work life gravitated to that field.

Meanwhile there were business drivers and self-determination drivers that motivated the developers of the manifesto to create and publish it. Since then, a body of work, practice, and set of cultural precepts have sprung up around the manifesto. But now we do have that body of work and history of experimentation to build on.

The motivators for self-determination and autonomy remain. The motivators for grappling with VUCA seem to constantly expand. Grappling effectively with a VUCA world requires the

Chapter 7: Your Own Agile Heart

development of internal complexity, which propels us forward in consciousness development.

Something Is Happening

In 2003, I was sitting inside the headquarters of the Bonneville Power Administration on a rare sunny Portland Saturday writing a software requirements specification for a new metering system. I had come late to the project after the first attempt had failed. There was a need for, not only clear requirements, but a higher degree of collaboration with the developers who were doing the coding. It was another instance of a great deal of overtime being required in order to catch up and turn the situation around. That floor of the BPA offices appeared to be completely empty. Something was preoccupying me. I moved from the keyboard to pen and paper, my preferred media for drafting poetry, and the following poured out on the page. Then, I went back to work.

Birth of the Rock Monster

There is a bed of rock--
bedrock.
And there is a deafening silence
in the little frightened crowd
as the bedrock shakes and trembles
and a subterranean shrieking--
LOUD
sunders the pleasing rock plain,
seemingly threatening the little crowd.

There is a monstrous rock giant
birthing itself from the plain
shrieking its joyful agony,
torn by its own birth pangs.

Your Life as Your Playground

For the self-birth is the hardest
and the little crowd must call it strange
when the rock giant rears free of its substance
and causes itself such pain.

Now the monster yanks it's head from the bedrock.
Now the creature shrugs the plain from its shoulders.
Now its chest rises above the population
as the plain reclaims bits of head and shoulders.
Now the beast without speech howls in joyful grief
as its hips rise above the desolation.
Now the desolate being is catapulted
free of rock plain, free of crowd,
into self-initiation.

Now the rock-beast without priest is christened
by the shouts and the screams of the onlookers.
Now the creature is shot free of its moorings,
leaving familiar rock, trailing bits of rock,
as it's shot from rock
toward the sun, toward the sky,
toward the morning.

And the only reminder as it wails out of sight
is the hole in the ground
where it wrenched free with its might.
And the only sound in the beast's own ears
is the sound of its own shrieking
as it confronts its own fears.

Years later, this poem exemplifies much of what I've seen in many agile adoptions. Agile rears up out of a great "stuckness" attended by a class of coaches, consultants and champions. It

Chapter 7: Your Own Agile Heart

metamorphoses into something these original advocates never truly imagined or created, and then is sustained or not, often in the face of much fear and methodological hostility from both the predictive and adaptive camps.

There seems to be a steady and rapidly gathering shift in the tide of agile-aspiring workplaces these days. Many companies have spent large amounts of money; the larger companies have spent into the tens of millions and years of their corporate lifecycles engaging consultants, paying for special tools and training in the pursuit of agility. Many have seen certain levels of success. But, many have not, and for many that have seen success, an influential champion leaves or time passes and the agile adoption loses steam as the traditions and consciousness of the dominant paradigm re-asserts itself. I've heard claims of up to 900% improvement in productivity made by some agile advocates, and I have worked with clients who've said that they had come to the point where they just about couldn't ship software at all until they started adopting agile methods and thinking. Agile has brought great gifts to some.

Occasionally, agile has carried water for the mistakes of others. A few years ago, I was contacted by a former client to come into the PMO to turn around a red agile project. I had previously coached Scrum Masters there in another part of the organization for over a year. But, one of the project managers, the manager of the Scrum Masters, and the director of the group the Scrum Masters reported into all knew that I also had a strong project management background. I spoke with the director of the PMO and started to work immediately.

Within days it became clear that, though the Scrum Master in place was not engaged or interested in facilitating the team and needed to find a new career horizon, it was also just as clear that the project was awry for other reasons. The PM had kept requesting money but there was no evidence of a high-level plan, charter, clear budget, or much other evidence of a project having been managed. The vendor of the system being implemented had taken the project over in a desperate attempt to stop their own financial bleed. Over $2 million had been spent. There was nothing ready to deliver, and further analysis showed that it would take another $2 million to deliver the first of three releases. Additionally, the business case for the project had evaporated while the project was meandering along. No one had noticed outside the team, and no one was listening to the team.

This was not a problem with agile methods, but there was a problem with leadership and clarity of the sponsor role on that project. A retrospective showed that the team had early on raised all the issues that had caused the project to founder, but they had been told to sit down and shut up. And so they did.

Sometimes, the agile champions are the problem. In a range of engagements over my years as an agile coach, I've seen internal agile champions who were not well versed in the agile framework they were applying actually undermining their objective to encourage the adoption of agile in their organization.

In another case, I was working with a global director of delivery who was a deeply impassioned agile advocate with a strong allegiance to "Scrum by the book." After agreeing that "the book" we could all align around was the Scrum Guide, we began to design an engagement that would assess the current state of practice across nine teams and particularly focus on one team that was having a lot of trouble.

As I observed this particular advocate struggle to communicate vision and set a context that would protect the teams, I saw not only the extent to which he was pressured to compromise the system in favor of the exigencies of delivery as his supervisor

Chapter 7: Your Own Agile Heart

saw them but also the extent to which he created the chaos that he was attempting to manage. This leader had a hard time being consistent in his messaging about focus, process, and accountability.

The most common example of this was that he would jump into a sprint and direct action at the team level when key delivery dates were looming. This sent a variety of contradictory messages about courage, commitment to process, actual level of autonomy, and even the team's ability to rely on his support. In a late evening three-way conversation with him, his supervisor, and myself, it became clear to me that he was under tremendous personal and professional pressure from his supervisor which was driving these behaviors. This agile champion was challenged beyond his skill to coach back to his supervisor or self-manage to reset the context he was in, a key factor in the demise of that agile adoption.

And, lastly, I find myself reflecting on the comments of a colleague who typically works with the C-Suite or high-ranking government officials. She said that these leaders are rarely aware of the amount of chaos they inject into the organizational systems they would say they lead. Leadership is sometimes part of the VUCA context. And, I'll say more about that in the appendix on pervasive leadership. Essentially, we, the led, collude in this when we do not shoulder our portion of the leadership burden.

Clearly, agile methods have become far more common in industry. But, often, it seems we think that walking through rituals will automagically transform an organization. Agile transformations are fundamentally personal transformations. I've heard it said that only 10% of any population needs to change to influence a shift in the whole population. It is necessary for agile coaches to be the first among that 10%. It is necessary that they walk within an agile consciousness to safeguard themselves against falling back down the ladder of their own development when the going gets tough.

Chapter 8: What You Can Do

Sometimes we go through periods of test and trial. If you've ever been part of or witnessed an agile adoption that's lost its heart and has become a hamster wheel of standups, forced planning sessions, followed by forced marches and precious little learning—or development—you know what I mean. Sometimes it seems there's something out there that has a wicked sense of humor, like a winter with a score to settle.

Ice Storm, 2004

Winter came to us ungently,
not in soft furs and frosty sighs
but naked, with ice for bones,
her gaunt hand clutching
at our collective throats.
She had no time or patience
for our weak-willed sniveling
but went about her business
with the purpose and assurance
of a crone who knows the way
to the bitter herbs that will save her people.
We soft-fleshed humans
railed at her swift disregard
for our petty routines.
Our homes became prisons
if we lacked the wisdom
to make them sanctuaries.
First beaten into a submission
appropriate to lesser, warm-blooded mortals,
some of us then lashed out
armored in Thinsulate and Gortex,

Ice Storm, 2004

challenging haughty Winter.
She ignored our rebellion,
being a higher power,
and went on freezing us,
layering us with ice and snow
for 66 human-stymying hours.
To her willing subjects
she brought a rich solitude,
a balm of silence in which to see
their world with new eyes
and themselves, as well.
And, when she felt we had had enough,
she let go her grip,
unveiled the lazy sun,
stepped back into anonymous "Nature,"
where she stands watching to see
whether the tincture of solitude
has had its effect.

What You Can Do

If you are interested in seeing the world be a better place for people as well as for businesses and customers, there are several things you can do.

First, know that even if the computer the Agile Manifesto and Principles is hosted on goes permanently offline, the agile values and principles will be around for a very long time. They are evidence of a romantic movement in industry that began in software development and focused on human experience in the workplace. They began to lever us out of the mechanistic Taylorism[****] that still pervades much of modern work in

---

[****] Taylorism is a model of management and work organization based on

Chapter 8: What You Can Do

organizations. Know that you, as an individual, have choice. Even in the darkest days of communism, there were thinkers in Czechoslovakia doing their thinking, writing, conferring, and living in a way that resulted in the Velvet Revolution, a peaceful transfer of power and downfall of the Czech communist regime in 1989[††††]. Then, as now, great change resulted from a few determined individuals. Be determined for yourself and those in your sphere of influence. Do your thinking and self-development; be a reader and a learner attentive to the kind of learning you are doing. Pursue a velvet revolution wherever you find yourself.

Second, make sure you have a large collection of "agile buddies," as I tell my clients. Some day we may not call these fellow travelers agilists anymore, but they are your likeminded crew who go along with you on this journey. Choose fellow travelers who are, indeed, still travelling. In this way, we go forward in the shelter of each other. You'll spot them by their ongoing personal development, their asking of good questions at least as much as providing answers. They may or may not be showing up at gatherings of agilists, but they will be reading and experimenting in their lives and work to improve the quality of their experience and their outcomes. Find them, open a feedback loop with them, and go along together.

Third, do not ever be afraid to learn more about the deep theory that is under all the repeatable process, methods, and models you'll hear agilists talk about. Digging into and understanding the theory is how you will be able to gain greater mastery of what agile is and when a system that is being labeled "agile" really isn't. And, act from that theory even when acting within a recognized framework. Fourth, and perhaps this should be first, work on yourself. Pursue

---

the work of Frederick Taylor (b. 1856 d. 1915). While the term "Taylorism" is familiar to many agilists, it's interesting to note that the alternative name for this approach is "scientific management."

†††† https://en.wikipedia.org/wiki/Velvet_Revolution

What You Can Do

your own development, not just learning. Be aware of the kind of learning opportunities that are coming your way. Be alert to whether you will be learning more technical information and getting better at known things without learning more about yourself or expanding the set of lenses you have to put on when you look out at the world or in at yourself. Consider on at least a yearly basis—birthdays and anniversaries are great for this—whether you have moved an inch along the path to increased internal complexity. Reflect on whether you have made any significant changes and reach out to others to ask whether your charming self-feedback is anywhere near the mark.

Fifth, know that we're all in this together, but you can't set anyone else on the developmental path. There are many researchers, academicians, and coaches who are working hard to figure out how we as adults can help other interested adults to truly develop. It's a hard thing, given the state of this world we have created. Our organizations and the conditions created in them are clear evidence of the level of development most of us are at. It's not helpful to compare pain, and it's not helpful to compare levels of development, particularly given how hard that is to do. But each of us can focus specific effort to develop and do good. By developing your degree of awareness of your context, the quality of your noticing, your knowledge and understanding of Self and Other you —can possibly be a fine example to some unknown observer. And this can make quite a bit of difference.

I have learned a lot from exploring. This does not mean I have never created a plan and followed it. For instance, I created an outline for this book—and then I went about modifying the outline as the book emerged. It would not have been the same book, and I don't think it would have been readable or useful if I'd stuck to the original outline. I encourage exploration. As I often tell people I coach or mentor about career concerns, "My career is my adventure. I hope yours is, too." So it is with the practical

Chapter 8: What You Can Do

and philosophical aspects of being our best selves and evolving a finer human operating system for the planet through our work in organizations. Agile adoptions are only sustainable if they are about waking up and growing up, and this is essentially a personal experience.

I wanted in this book to acknowledge your experience by sharing mine and my observations. I hope it's been of use to you. I'd like to leave you with this poem by way of encouragement.

What's Necessary

What's necessary
is to get to the heart of the matter.
Yet, each time I arrive there
I see a light further down the corridor,
hear a small voice saying
"But, wait! There are greater riches
further along."
Blinded by the whole of you
I cannot pick out one part
to praise first.

Appendix A: Why Work?

This book essentially poses the question: As an agilist, what will you do with your one precious life?

The work of evolving your own consciousness is neither easy nor trivial. It's very difficult. Being an agile advocate who presides over or participates in a failed or flagging agile adoption is also not easy. It's worth asking why you put yourself in this situation in the first place. Consider thinking this through. The questions below may help

Questions for Contemplation and Self-Clarification

What are your values around work? Is it just a paycheck for you? If so, that's fine, but it's worthwhile knowing that about yourself. And, know that, some days, that's what it is for most people. This question asks how you feel about your purpose in working *overall*.

Questions for Contemplation and Self-Clarification

What do you hope to gain or achieve by pursuing agility in your life or the organization you serve? Does agile interest you for personal or societal reasons?

Appendix A: Why Work?

If you could do something else with your life, what would it be? If you can answer this with something other than being an agile coach or advocate, perhaps it's time to go do that thing? And, if it isn't, why not? For many people, this work is too personally difficult to do for long, even if well-compensated, unless you also have other motivators.

Appendix B: Theory U Principles and Practices

This appendix provides a brief overview of the principles and practices which animate Theory U. All page references refer to pages in Theory U: Leading from the Future as It *Emerges*: The Social Technology of Presencing. This appendix is meant to be a scannable overview of the content there. The pages are referenced here so that you may jump into wherever you are intrigued in that book. To be honest, I'd recommend reading the whole thing cover to cover because it leaves you with a firm grounding in what a social technology is and why we need to use the term intentionally.

Co-Initiating Principle

• Attend: Listen to what life calls you to do (Scharmer, 2009, pp. 379-380).
• Connect: Listen to and dialogue with interesting players in the field (pp. 380-384).
• Co-initiate a diverse core group that inspires a common intention (pp. 384- 387).

Co-Sensing Principle

• Form a highly committed prototyping core team and clarify essential questions (pp. 387-389).
• Take deep-dive journeys to the places of most potential (pp. 389-393).
• Observe, observe, observe: Suspend your Voice of Judgement (VOJ) and connect with your sense of wonder (pp. 393-394).
• Practice deep listening and dialogue: Connect to others with your mind, heart, and will wide open (pp. 394-398).
• Create collective sensing organs that allow the system to see itself (pp. 398-399).

Co-Presencing Principle

Co-Presencing Principle

- Letting go: Let go of your old self and "stuff" that must die (pp. 399-401).
- Letting come: Connect and surrender to the future that wants to emerge through you (pp. 401-402).
- Intentional silence: Pick a practice that helps you to connect to your source (pp. 402-407).
- Follow your journey: Do what you love, love what you do (pp. 407-410).
- Circles of Presence: Create circles in which you hold one another in the highest future intention (pp. 410-412).

Co-Creating Principle

- The Power of Intention: Connect to the future that stays in need of you—crystallize your vision and intention (pp. 412-415).
- Form core groups: Five people can change the world (pp. 415-416).
- Prototype strategic microcosms as a landing strip for the emerging future (pp. 416-421).
- Integrate head, heart, and hand: Seek it with your hands; don't think about it, feel it (pp. 421-423).
- Iterate, iterate, iterate: create, adapt, and always be in dialogue with the universe (pp. 424-425).

Co-Evolving Principle
- Co-evolve innovation ecosystems that allow people to see and act from an emerging whole (pp. 426-430).
- Create innovation infrastructures by shaping safe places and rhythms for peer coaching (supported through social technology) (pp. 430-434).
- Social Presencing Theater: Evolve collective awareness through Field 4 media productions (pp. 434-436).

Appendix B: Theory U Principles and Practices

Root Principles Which Contain Three Groundings

- Intentional grounding (pp. 436-438).
- Relational grounding (pp. 438-439).
- Authentic grounding (pp. 439-441).

Appendix C: Pervasive Leadership

At various points in this book, I have referred to Pervasive Leadership. This is a leadership model I began developing as I was working on my master's thesis in the early 2000s. Increasingly, I have found that exposing software teams to Pervasive Leadership has immediate benefits. We seem to have forgotten that we were all born with the same power within us. We have become so enculturated to giving our power over to others in exchange for a false promise of safety, that we have nearly snuffed out our own light. All too often, we wait to be permitted, told what to do, or guided by someone who has more positional power, thereby abdicating the use of our own authentic power.

All too often, those leaders we wait on don't—and can't possibly—have the answers we seek. The problem sets, even in small organizations, are too large and varied requiring too much specific and varied technical information to be addressed for most nominal leaders to address for us.

This leadership model has two primary goals. First, it is designed to increase agility by decreasing decision latency and increasing decision quality across the organization. This is accomplished by improving everyone's ability to see decision points as they arise, determine whether they are best handled at their local level, and rapidly communicate out the decision point, the decision, and the results. This means that managers are no longer authority figures—most of the time, but that they are now coaching these skills into all their direct reports. Second, it is designed to support personal growth that can feed personal transformation, which is a key theme in this book.

Appendix C: Pervasive Leadership

The Principles

Pervasive Leadership requires that adherents follow these principles:

Change your mental model of I and Thou.

Pervasive leaders see themselves as being in a dialogue with everyone in their work group, or, if the organization is small enough, everyone in their organization. They have something to learn and something of value to offer. Where they are granted power-over authority, they use it extremely rarely. They have learned to function in a way that makes that kind of authority largely unnecessary.

Act locally; think holistically.

Pervasive leaders realize that patterns and problems they see in their immediate work group are also likely arising elsewhere in the organization. They solve them locally and offer the solution to the larger organization. They also seek solutions elsewhere because someone else may have spotted and solved the problem first. Their objective is always to help the organization move forward and fulfill its stated purpose as fully as possible as quickly as possible.

Enact empathetic stewardship.

Pervasive leaders realize the importance of empathy and the risks of compassion fatigue. They realize also that, while each individual is uniquely valuable, the organization as a whole is the ship we all travel in, so they are careful to advocate for the needs of the organization in balance with the needs of the individual.

Appendix D: Responsive

On April 17, 2017, I was on a panel at a Meetup in Portland, Oregon that was a fishbowl conversation across three communities interested in "the future of work." Those communities were the lean, agile, and responsive communities. The fishbowl panel functioned such that three of us representing the three different communities sat in the center surrounded by the audience. The facilitator ensured that talking time was balanced and that we stayed on track. Our purpose was to determine whether these three communities had the skill and will to talk across boundaries to explore their similarities and differences and to possibly find synergy among their interests. It went remarkably well, and as a result, as a I write this, I am sitting on a steering committee formed to create an Open Space conference on the topic of the future of work next year.

However, what was interesting to me was the apparent progression across time of the focus on dynamic adjustment around work outcomes and process in organization while focusing on human experience and organizational sustainability. It was almost as though each community had built on the successes and tried to mitigate the gaps in the thrust of the previous community where the human experience was concerned. First the lean, then the agile, and now the responsive community is trying to do good for people while doing well in organizational outcomes and financial sustainability. It was surprising to me how similar to the agile movement the springing forth of the Responsive movement had been. Their manifesto even looked much like the Agile Manifesto.

A Recapitulation of the Responsive Manifesto

To support your exploration of the world around you, I'll recapitulate the Responsive manifesto here. You may find fellow travelers there.

A Recapitulation of the Responsive Manifesto

Everyone and everything is connected.

The world has become one giant network where instantly accessible and shareable information rewrites the future as quickly as it can be understood. Fueled by relentless technological innovation, this accelerating connectivity has created an ever increasing rate of change. As a result, the future is becoming increasingly difficult to predict.

Meanwhile, most organizations still rely on a way of working designed over 100 years ago for the challenges and opportunities of the industrial age. Team structures support routine and static jobs. Siloed, command and control systems enable senior leadership to drive efficiency and predictability at the expense of free information flow, rapid learning, and adaptability.

The tension between organizations optimized for predictability and the unpredictable world they inhabit has reached a breaking point.

Organizations are struggling to keep up with their customers. Workers caught between dissatisfied customers and uninspiring leaders are becoming disillusioned and disengaged. Executives caught between discontented investors and disruptive competitors are struggling to find a path forward. And people who want a better world for themselves and their communities are looking to new ambitious organizations to shape our collective future.

We need a new way.

Responsive Organizations are built to learn and respond rapidly through the open flow of information; encouraging experimentation and learning on rapid cycles; and organizing as a network of employees, customers, and partners motivated by shared purpose

Appendix D: Responsive

What is a Responsive Org?

There's a reason we've run organizations the way we have. Our old Command and Control operating model was well-suited for complicated and predictable challenges. Some of these challenges still exist today and may respond to the industrial-era practices that we know so well. However, as the pace of change accelerates, the challenges we face are becoming less and less predictable. Those practices that were so successful in the past are counter-productive in less predictable environments. In contrast, Responsive Organizations are designed to thrive in less predictable environments by balancing the following tensions:

More Predictable ←→ Less Predictable

Profit ←→ Purpose
Hierarchies ←→ Networks
Controlling ←→ Empowering
Planning ←→ Experimentation
Privacy ←→ Transparency

To learn more about Responsive go to responsive.org. There is much clarification there.

Glossary

Below is a short glossary of terms that may be new to some readers of this book.

Action Learning
A learning approach that involves active experimentation and design of activities that generate real work products as part of the learning experience.

Consciousness
A quality of awareness, noticing, and knowledge of self and other.

Dialogic stance
A way of positioning yourself, or presencing, in interactions with others that is based on curiosity, intent to learn, intent to express your needs, and a focus on listening for the other person's point of view.

Dialogue
A form of conversation between humans that involves give and take, a listening style that seeks to understand the other person from their point of view, respectful advocacy for one's own viewpoint, and inquiry based on curiosity about the other's viewpoint.

Perspective taking
The process of "standing in another person's shoes," or attempting to see the world from another perspective.

Power-Over
A relationship between two people or groups of people where one has or exerts power over the other. This is a characteristic of competitive interactions and authoritarian relationships.

Power-With
A relationship between two or more people or groups of
people where power is not only balanced but typically used
for mutual benefit. This is a characteristic of collaboration and
facilitative relationships.

Recommended Reading

Argyris, C. (1991) Teaching Smart People How To Learn. Harvard Business Review 4(5): 4-15

Argyris, C. (1994) Good Communication That Blocks Learning. (cover story). Harvard Business Review, 72(4), 77. Retrieved from EBSCOhost.

Argyris, C. (2002) Double-Loop Learning, Teaching, and Research. Academy of Management Learning & Education, 1(2), 206-218. doi:10.5465/AMLE.2002.8509400

Denning, S. (2010) *The Leader's Guide to Radical Management.* San Francisco: John Wiley & Sons, Inc.

Greenleaf, R. (1991) Servant Leadership: A Journey into the Nature of Legitimate Power and Greatness. Mahwah, NJ: Paulist Press.

Hamel, G. (2007) *The Future of Management.* (2009). Boston: Harvard Business School Press.

Heifetz, R., Grashow, A., Linsky, M.. (2009) *The Practice of Adaptive Leadership: Tools and Tactics for Changing Your Organization and the World.* Boston: Harvard Business Press.

Hock, D. (2000a) The Art of Chaordic Leadership. Leader to Leader, 2000(15), 20-26. Retrieved from Business Source Complete database.

Hock, D. (2000b) Birth of the Chaordic Age. Executive Excellence, 17(6), 6. Retrieved from MasterFILE Premier database.

Laloux, F. (2015) *Reinventing Organizations*. Brussels: Nelson Parker.

McKenna, J. (2014) *Conscious Software Development.* CreateSpace Independent Publishing Platform.

McNamara, R. (2013) *The Elegant Self: A Radical Approach to Personal Evolution for Greater Influence in Life.* Boulder: Performance Integral.

McTaggert, L. (2008) *The Field: The Quest for the Secret Force of the Universe.* New York: Harper.

Midgley, M. (2001) *Science and Poetry.* London: Routledge Classics.

Mills, A. (2016) *Everyone is a Change Agent: A Guide to the Change Agent Essentials.* Cornelius: Createspace.

Mindell, A. Ph.D. (1992) *The Leader as Martial Artist: Techniques and Strategies for Resolving Conflict and Creating Community.* San Francisco: Harper.

Neiman, S. (2015) *Why Grow Up?: Subversive Thoughts for an Infantile Age.* New York: Farrar, Straus and Giroux.

Patterson, K. et al (2013) *Crucial Accountability: Tools for Resolving Violated Expectations, Broken Commitments, and Bad Behavior, 2nd edition.* New York: McGraw Hill Education

Richardson, J. (2014) *Double Loop Learning: A Powerful Force for Organizational Excellence.* Pacific Northwest Software Quality Conference Proceedings 2014.

Recommended Reading

Senge, P., Scharmer, C. O., Jaworski, J., & Flowers, B. S.
(2004b) *Presence: An Exploration Of Profound
Change In People, Organizations, And Society.*
New York: Currency Doubleday.

Sennett, R. (1999) *The Corrosion Of Character: The Personal
Consequences Of Work In The New Capitalism.*
New York: W. W. Norton.

Wheatley, M. J. (1999) *Leadership and the New Science:
Discovering Order in a Chaotic World.*
San Francisco, CA: Berrett-Koehler Publishers, Inc.

Whyte, D. (2009) *The Three Marriages: Reimagining Work, Self
And Relationship.* New York: Riverhead Books.

Author Biography

Jean Richardson is an agile coach and consultant as well as a poet who lives in Portland, Oregon. She also provides training, coaching, and turnaround leadership on troubled projects and programs.

She first studied poetry under Jim Bodeen at A.C. Davis High School in Yakima, Washington. His influence was indelible. She first published poetry through Copper Canyon Press in 1979 in a collection of broadsides named Miso Soup. Her contributions were "The Veil", a poem about a misbegotten wedding, and "Listen to My Father Talk of Cattle", about a family drive through a US Government firing range where war games were played with live ammunition each summer near her childhood home. She went on to publish in The Ellensburg Anthology (1983, 1984, 1985), Weathered Pages: The Poetry Pole (2005, Blue Begonia Press), and Quartet: Four Poetic Voices (2006, Media Weavers, LLC). She writes far more than she attempts to publish because submission has never been her bailiwick.

As well as being an agile coach and turnaround leader, Jean has taught at the Oregon Graduate Institute, Portland State University, and Marylhurst University. She coaches people in roles from the individual contributor level to the executive level. She has been a volunteer mediator in the Multnomah County Court Small Claims, and earlier, landlord/tenant court since 9/11. She has also served as a Better Business Bureau Oregon Lemon Law arbitrator. She finds the process of humans working themselves out through conversation transfixing. Jean offers public speaking, coaching, training, and turnaround leadership services through Azure Gate Consulting, LLC.

Jean also provides individual coaching to Scrum Masters, agile coaches, and managers in transition to an agility-supporting leadership stance.

Engagement details can be found at https://www.azuregate.net/individual-coaching/.

Endnotes

[1] Carreira, J. Radical Inclusivity: *Expanding Our Minds Beyond Dualistic Thinking.* Philadelphia: Emergence Education. P. 12.

[2] Modern Agile was introduced by its creator, Joshua Kerievsky, CEO of Industrial Logic, at Agile2016, a conference sponsored by the Agile Alliance. You can view the keynote here https://www.agilealliance.org/resources/videos/modern-agile/, and you can learn more about Modern Agile at http://modernagile.org/.

[3] Richardson, J. and Plavcan, M. Technical Practices as a Hack on Consciousness, InfoQ.com, September 1, 2016 https://www.infoq.com/articles/technical-hack-conciousness

[4] Stiehm, J. *U.S. Army War College: Military Education In A Democracy.* Temple University Press, Sep 23, 2010. P. 128.

[5] Oliver, M. "The Summer Day." *New and Selected Poems*, 1992, Boston: Beacon Press.

[6] https://www.linkedin.com/pulse/what-ineffable-agile-jean-richardson

[7] Roethke, T. "The Waking," *The Collected Poems of Theodore Roethke.* Garden City: Anchor/Double Day. 1975. P. 104.

[8] Rose, C. (Executive Producer). (2007, August 10). Charlie Rose: An hour with John Rigas (Television broadcast). New York: Charlie Rose LLC.

[9] http://www.oregonlive.com/silicon-forest/index.ssf/2016/04/intel_layoffs_heres_what_emplo.html

[10] https://www.linkedin.com/pulse/what-ineffable-agile-jean-richardson

[11] Whyte, D. (1994). *The heart aroused: Poetry and the preservation of the soul in corporate America. New York: Currency Doubleday.* P. 147.

[12] Whyte, 1994, p. 182

[13] Whyte, 1994, p. 183

[14] Richardson, J. and Plavcan, M. Technical Practices as a Hack on Consciousness, InfoQ, September 1, 2016 https://www.infoq.com/articles/technical-hack-conciousness

[15] https://www.infoq.com/articles/technical-hack-conciousness

[16] https://youtu.be/iD4HybKFb24

[17] http://stateofagile.versionone.com/

[18] 11th Annual State of Agile Report. VersionOne. http://stateofagile.versionone.com/ P. 12.

[19] Godin, Seth, "Stop Stealing Dreams," https://youtu.be/sXpbONjV1Jc

[20] 11th Annual State of Agile Report. VersionOne. http://stateofagile.versionone.com/ P. 13.

[21] 11th Annual State of Agile Report. VersionOne. http://stateofagile.versionone.com/ P. 13.

[22] Page 8.

Endnotes

[23] Page 9.

[24] https://explore.versionone.com/state-of-agile/versionone-11th-annual-state-of-agile-report-2
https://hbr.org/2016/05/embracing-agile
https://hbr.org/product/managing-the-transition-to-the-new-agile-business-and-product-development-model-lessons-from-cisco-systems/BH770-PDF-ENG
https://hbr.org/2016/10/make-your-strategy-more-agile
https://www.accenture.com/us-en/insight-government-agile-ready
https://www.accenture.com/us-en/insight-breathing-agility-into-pharmaceutical-industry
https://www.accenture.com/us-en/blogs/blogs-want-grow-your-market-share
Four Keys to Organizational Agility: From Agile to Agility, Cutter Agile Product & Project Management Volume 14, Number 3.

[25] http://azuregate.net/resources/?preview_id=94&preview_nonce=0c8cefa6ae&preview=true#UsefulVideos Note that this video is difficult to view on modern playback devices. You can attain a copy by contacting the author directly.

[26] Combs, A. (2009). Consciousness Explained Better: To wards an Integral Understanding of the Multifaceted Nature of Consciousness. St Paul: Paragon House. Page 117.

[27] Richardson, J and Plavcan, M. "Technical Practices as a Hack on Consciousness" InfoQ. https://www.infoq.com/articles/technical-hack-conciousness

[28] Mkenna, J. *Conscious Software Development*, Location 277 in the Kindle edition.

[29] Birth of the Chaordic Age, page 117.

[30] Davies, R. *Tempest Tost* Vol. 1 of *The Salterton Trilogy*. P. 116.

[31] Greenleaf, R. K. (1991). Servant Leadership: A Journey into the Nature of Legitimate Power and Greatness. "Servant As Leader." Mahwah, NJ: Paulist Press.

[32] Peschl, M. "Triple-loop learning as foundation for profound change, individual cultivation, and radical innovation. Construction processes beyond scientific and rational knowledge." Constructivist Foundations 2(2-3). P. 138.

[33] Peschle, M. P. 138.

[34] Scharmer, P. 96.

[35] Nicolaides, A. and McCallum, D. "Inquiry in Action for Leadership in Turbulent Times: Exploring the Connections Between Transformative Learning and Adaptive Leadership" in Journal of Transformative Education. Pgs. 246 – 260. DOI: 10.1177/1541344614540333

[36] Nicolaides and McCallum, P. 255.

[37] Simon, S. "They'd Trade Labor Day for Days of Labor." National Public Radio Weekend Edition Sunday, http://www.npr.org/templates/story/story.php?storyId=129647232

[38] Kilmann, R. H. & Thomas, K. W. (2007). *Thomas-Kilmann Conflict Mode Instrument*. Mountain View, CA: Consulting Psychologists Press, Inc.